Compensation $ense 101

Common Sense Answers to Your Questions About Employee Compensation and Total Rewards

CASSANDRA FAUROTE, CCP, SPHR, SHRM-SCP

ISBN-13: 978-1-7326635-0-3

DEDICATION

This book is dedicated to my husband, Terry. As I often tell you, "Thank you so much for letting me do *me*." Not only are you a huge supporter; you also make it possible for me to be the best version of myself and follow my passion daily.
You are simply the best!

And to my children, Brannon and Abby. You allow me to be both a mother and a business owner. I hope I have shown you that you can follow your passion and be a participatory and involved parent at the same time. I love you both deeply, and you are why I want to be who I am and why I want to achieve what I can in this lifetime.

And to Kim, my best friend forever. You have been my biggest supporter from the very beginning as I started my business. You are my one of my best encouragers and you continue to support what I do every day.

CONTENTS

ACKNOWLEDGMENTS

I could not have completed this book without the great support and help from my editor, Bob Chenoweth. You have assisted me with my writing for so many years now, and you always help me put my best foot forward. Thank you for your work on this book and the many other publications on which we've collaborated.

I also wish to thank Shellye Kaplin, Susan Kaspar, and Amanda Parker and her team for supporting me for so many years in this business endeavor. Each of you helps us deliver the best compensation services to our clients.

There are also many amazing strategic partners, friends, and family who send us referrals and support our business on a regular basis. I am so thankful to each of you for enabling us to build this business as we support you and your referrals.

FOREWORD

Today, offering competitive compensation – much less competitive total rewards – is simply your organization's "ticket to play" in the high-stakes talent wars. Free food and "Bring Your Dog to Work Day" events are nice, but they don't pay the rent. As the talent pool tightens, what once worked to attract entry level employees may not be enough to empower your organization to win in today's talent competition. Indeed, compensation is the foundation on which other benefits are built. Without competitive compensation, those employee engagement-focused benefits will be ineffective as recruiting and retention tools.

Ask a senior Human Resources (HR) leader, "What is your area of weakness?" and often the response will be "Compensation." Indeed, compensation is its own area of expertise. To be truly good in this area requires years of experience and a willingness to dig deep into data – and then compare it to yet more data. Most of us do not have the patience or the skill to do much more than make a good guess about compensation for a few straightforward positions. But really, how many positions are "straightforward" these days? Yes, we can articulate a compensation philosophy, but we still need to bring in experts when it comes to evaluating whether our organization's compensation is competitive.

Even if you plan to bring in a compensation consultant, however, you need a basic level of compensation knowledge to ensure you can provide information the consultant needs, and that you understand your options when making decisions with your consultant. Reading this book will give you that fundamental knowledge.

What are the right questions to ask? How can you be sure you are looking at compensation from the right perspective? Is an incentive plan reasonable for your organization? What if you want to motivate your sales team? What if your compensation structure is equitable across the organization based on tenure, but not for race or gender? How can you be certain your organization is being compliant with regulations? Are the rules different for a nonprofit? How much is enough – and how much is too much – of a bonus to offer a senior executive? How does compensation differ by industry or sector?

continued

1

Answering these and other questions requires expertise developed over many years serving clients from a broad spectrum of industries. Compensation and total rewards expert Cassandra Faurote has the depth of experience needed, and the ability, to simplify the mystique of compensation. She knows what trends lie on the horizon and whether they are appropriate for your organization.

Whether you are a seasoned C-suite executive or a generalist early in your career as a compensation and total rewards professional, you will benefit from this practical guide. Certainly, understanding how to use compensation and total rewards as a competitive advantage has never been more important!

That's why Cassandra has written *Compensation $ense 101: Common Sense Answers to Your Questions About Employee Compensation and Total Rewards*. She understands the questions organizations need to address and she has the answers – for you.

Nancy S. Ahlrichs, SPHR, SHRM-SCP
Chief Talent Officer, United Way of Central Indiana

JUST FOR FUN:
10 STUPID WAYS WE DEAL WITH EMPLOYEE COMPENSATION*

#10 – We let employees scare us with irrelevant data from the internet.

#9 – We don't think pay makes a difference.

#8 – We don't tell employees how their pay compares to market.

#7 – We give all employees the same annual increase percentage (aka the "peanut butter approach").

#6 – We don't do a good job identifying top performers or top talent.

#5 – We don't use rewards and recognition and we think small increases are enough.

#4 – We see compensation as an expense and not an investment.

#3 – We try to solve all management problems with compensation.

#2 – We think staff members are going to stay put and do not have opportunities elsewhere.

#1 – We simply don't do *anything!!!*

To avoid falling into these (and more) employee compensation traps, take total rewards seriously. First step: Read the rest of this book!

*Created with Debi Mueller of Mueller Consulting Group

INTRODUCTION

Compensation is one of many facets of the overall Human Resources (HR) function in a business environment. Indeed, there are several areas within the scope of compensation, as well as many other areas of HR that are affected by compensation, as this illustration shows:

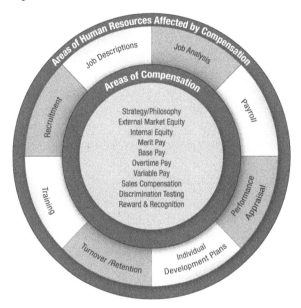

Well-crafted compensation solutions help your organization by providing many key benefits. These include the following:

- Appropriate pay ranges for recruitment
- Accurate job descriptions
- A basis for determining external value of a position to market
- Identification of who is eligible to receive overtime pay
- A foundation for reviewing employee performance and rewarding the right behaviors
- An indication of skills gaps and training needs
- Improved employee morale and engagement, which can help reduce turnover

Naturally, there are many more benefits to proper compensation programs. But well-crafted compensation solutions are also about ethics and integrity. First, providing fair and equitable employee compensation is the right thing to do. Second, it is the law, and being in compliance can reduce severe financial and Public Relations (PR) risk for your organization! Beyond this, properly designed, implemented and managed compensation programs are simply good business. They engage employees, bolster job satisfaction, and help drive a better bottom line. In fact, I started my business because it is my passion to help employers achieve all these goals.

The problem most people face with compensation is that it seems like the proverbial "black box". In other words, it is both mysterious and misunderstood. With that in mind, it has always been my mission to educate clients and others about employee compensation and total rewards when I can. And from that mission, this book was born. It is my wish, goal, and belief that this book will be an informative cover-to-cover read or a handy and helpful topic-by-topic reference source when needed.

So, I've organized this book in eight main chapters, each presented in a question-and-answer format. If you need information on Incentive Plans, for example, you'll find answers to common questions focused on that subject there. This holds true topic by topic and chapter by chapter. Between that logical arrangement and the content preview at the beginning of each chapter , you should be able to quickly find the information and answers you need.

Compensation $ense 101 is the culmination of my more than 25 years of HR experience, including many years specializing in compensation and well over a decade as an external compensation consultant.

In my company, Total Reward Solutions, we often ask, "Are your employees an investment or an expense?" It is my hope that you find your employees are indeed an investment, and that you will invest in your own knowledge with the help of this easy Q and A book.

Compensate Fairly!

Cassandra Faurote

*"If you pick the right people
and give them the opportunity
to spread their wings and
put compensation as a carrier behind it
you almost don't have to manage them."*

Jack Welch, Legendary American Executive, Author,
and Founder of the Jack Welch Management Institute

Compensation Administration

In this section you will learn about...

The Compensation Life Cycle

The Compensation Philosophy

The Market Pricing Policy

Budgeting for Compensation

The Total Rewards Strategy

Salary Surveys

Market Data

NOTE: Terms in *red italics* in the following text are defined in the Glossary.

What is *compensation administration?* Compensation administration involves continuous HR oversight or management of everything from compensation philosophy to market data to compensation budgets.

Why is compensation administration important? It is important because it sets the groundwork and continues to frame your compensation program. It is through compensation administration that you will make important decisions that guide your ongoing compensation processes.

What is the strategic life cycle of compensation? The strategic *compensation life cycle* correlates various aspects of compensation to attraction, engagement and retention.

For example, when your organization is in attraction mode, it mainly focuses on base pay unless you are filling a salesperson role or a position with a larger amount of variable pay. Managers or executives would be examples of employees in such positions.

continued

Incentive compensation is utilized when your organization is focused on engagement. If goals are set appropriately and within the line of sight (that is, on those activities an employee can truly affect), your incentive pay plans can help drive employee engagement.

And finally, when your organization is in retention mode, your focus is on your reward and recognition programs. Properly designed reward and recognition programs acknowledge and reward employees in ways that motivate the employees to remain with your organization.

 **What is a Total Rewards Strategy and why is it important?**

Organizations today must go beyond competitive compensation and benefit programs to compete for and retain talent. *Total rewards* help accomplish that because they encompass everything an employee values in their employment relationship.

Your *Total Rewards Strategy* MUST BE UNIQUE to your organization and the workforce you want to attract and retain. In other words, if you want to stand out, you can't merely do what everyone else is doing.

For example, beyond baseline compensation and benefits, Learning and Development programs, flexible working arrangements, and fun office perks may help differentiate you from your competition.

Built from your *people strategy* (which must define the resources and capabilities needed to execute the *business strategy*), your total rewards strategy should include competencies needed to support business objectives. To facilitate that, your organization's leadership must define the behaviors and skills required for the *"to be" model*, and how to bridge identified gaps from the *"as is" workforce*.

10

Aligning your people strategy with your business strategy affects how workers are deployed. Thus, your people strategy should be defined *after* your business strategy. Here's how some of the important strategic pieces connect:

- The *business strategy* provides the roadmap to the overall business direction.

- Your *Mission Statement* describes the business purpose – what you do, who you do it for, and how you do it.

- Your stated *Corporate Vision* presents your forward-thinking and desired future.

The business strategy is just the beginning. Unfortunately, most companies stop there. Oftentimes, executives spend days developing the business strategy but do not take it to the next level and define the necessary people strategy and total rewards strategy. It is crucial to take the time to align all three. By doing so, you can properly allocate limited budgets to align competencies and behaviors with those business outcomes that support the business strategy.

Why do I need a *Compensation Philosophy*, and how do I determine one for my organization?

Your *Compensation Philosophy* will define where your company wants to position itself compared to market. In other words, will you position your organization less than market, at market, or above market? This position doesn't have to be universal across your organization; you may need or desire a different Compensation Philosophy for various divisions or employee segments.

To make the right Compensation Philosophy decisions, it is important to ask the right questions regarding your organization and workforce. For example, is it easy for you to attract talent? If so, your compensation philosophy can probably be in line with market standards.

11

continued

Or do you have pockets where talent is scarce? If so, you might need a stronger compensation philosophy for hard-to-fill positions. And lastly, how do you want to structure your pay mix (base and variable) relative to market for those eligible for incentive compensation, bonuses and commissions?

To address these questions and properly design your compensation philosophy, start with a *Total Rewards Philosophy* that addresses cash compensation and benefits and how you want to utilize them (e.g., more cash than benefits or vice versa). You should then create a statement that addresses your culture. And finally, you may want to address the organization's philosophy in balancing social and fiscal responsibility.

Your philosophy for total rewards should be written down and shared with management and employees. In addition to a Total Rewards Philosophy, you may also want a separate *Compensation* Philosophy and a separate *Benefits Philosophy*. The Compensation Philosophy would go into more detail about your culture on compensation, your focus on base or total cash, what position you target in the market, and from where you rely on data.

Your Benefits Philosophy might go into more detail about how you want to position your benefits to market, how much choice you want to provide, if you will emphasize wellness, and from where you get comparator data for benefits.

Q **Should I participate in *salary surveys?***

A Whether to participate in *salary surveys* depends on the size of your organization and if you have adequate staff with time available to complete the surveys. Thus, large organizations with a dedicated compensation team will often participate in salary surveys, while smaller or medium-sized organizations often opt to get their data from compensation consultants (as this saves them time and cost, especially considering they might not have time to sufficiently evaluate the resulting salary data report).

12

Q If I participate in salary survey submissions, what do I need to do?

A Before you start downloading data and submitting it, consider completing the following steps:

1. Review any job descriptions that have changed in the last year to see if survey matches should change.

2. Ensure you have job descriptions for all new jobs created since the last time you completed survey submissions, so you might match those new jobs against your survey matches.

3. Clean up outdated job descriptions so you can do accurate *survey matching*. You may want to put each department, division, or even a few of each on a regular update schedule so job descriptions are reviewed and reapproved every one to two years.

Salary survey submissions can be time consuming. Therefore, weigh the time it takes to complete your data submission to receive a lower survey cost versus utilizing an outside consultant who has data readily available.

Q What is a *Market Pricing Policy?*

A Your *Market Pricing Policy* is your guide for how you will use the salary survey data once you get it back. It should address by job level (i.e., non-exempt, professional/technical, supervisor, manager, etc.) the scopes of data you will use from the survey to benchmark your jobs. The market pricing policy typically includes scopes for:

- Number of employees
- Revenue or asset size
- Geographic area for data comparisons
- Use of generic or industry-specific data

While number of employees and revenue or asset size scopes of data will remain the same for all job levels, the geographic area and use of generic or industry specific data scopes may vary by job level.

13

continued

You should also use your data to validate your current salary structure. Don't forget to "age" your data when you receive it as many months will likely have passed from when you submitted your data to when you receive your results.

Q How should I use the salary survey data?

A Use your survey data to see if market data correlating to any of your positions have moved up or down compared to the last time you received survey data. If so, decide what action you will take, including moving positions up or down in your pay grades. Also, apply your market data to your employee data. Look at your employees' base pay data as well as total cash data relative to your desired market position. Additionally, review your actual pay mix versus market pay mix. Once you know your position to market in base pay and total cash, you will be able to roll your data up by employee level, department, division, or even on a corporate level.

Q Do I need to "age" the market data? If so, how do I do that?

A Yes, don't forget to age your data before you apply it. To age your data, determine how many months have passed between your survey submission and when you are utilizing the data. Let's say it has been 6 months. You will need to determine what your industry merit movement average percentage is. Let's say it is 2.5%. Divide the 6 months that have passed by 12 months (in this case 6 divided by 12 = .5. Then multiply that number by the industry merit movement amount. Thus, using our example of 2.5% you would take .5 times 2.5, resulting in 1.25. That is the number you will turn into a decimal to use to age the data. In this example then, 1.25 would become 1.0125 for trending purposes. If a salary in the survey was $30,000, the decimal factor of 1.0125 would trend the data to $30,375.

The data aging in the above example was easy; the more months that pass between data submission and its application can make the aging process more complex. It is highly recommended you never age the data more than two years. At that point the data is becoming too old and may result in aging that is either too high or too low. It is best to obtain fresh market data annually.

How do I budget for compensation?

You will want to establish a budget for merit pay, equity pay, promotional/career development pay, bonuses, and other miscellaneous pay items. You can establish separate line items for each area or put them all together in one budget. It is important to consider all areas of compensation when budgeting or you may run out of money. Separate line item tracking is more accurate and ensures that dollars are budgeted appropriately for each area.

Let's address what to consider in each area as you develop your compensation budget:

Merit

Consider both external and internal factors when determining your merit budget. Internally, consider the following:

- What your organization can afford
- Your market competitiveness position (where do you sit as an organization relative to market)
- Benefit improvements you are making
- Technology improvements you are making
- Additional training you are funding

From an external perspective, consider the average market increase for your industry. However, you should not merely set your merit budget amount where the average merit increase is in the market. Rather, once you have evaluated all internal and external factors, then determine your merit budget.

continued

15

Equity

These budget dollars are used to increase compensation for employee positions where the market has moved significantly and employee pay is falling too far behind. These are also referred to as market increases; and these funds can also be used to correct any discrimination pay issues or internal equity issues (how employees compare to another in the same or like roles). To determine the equity budget needed, most organizations rely on how many dollars they have historically needed each year to correct equity issues; or will use market benchmarking, internal equity analysis and discrimination analysis findings.

Promotional/Career Development

Most organizations budget about ½ to 1% of total salaries to fund traditional promotions and/or career development pay. Traditional promotions typically result in a pay grade change whereas career development pay rewards employees for increasing skills and responsibilities but may not necessitate a grade change.

Bonuses

Some organizations budget for bonuses at the 100% target payout amount. Others will budget on the percent of target that has been historically paid out. Either way, it is important to assess quarterly the percent of target bonuses to ensure there are enough dollars being budgeted. If the organization is having an extremely good year and you determine at the end of quarter three that bonuses are going to pay out at 110% or 120%, you might need to increase your budget line for bonuses at that time.

Other Pay

And finally, consider all other types of pay and budget for them as well. Examples would be sign-on bonuses, guaranteed draws, shift differentials, geographic differentials, and hazard pay.

Base Pay

In this section you will learn about...

Base Pay Programs

Direct and Indirect Compensation

Market Data Guidelines

Job Analysis

Market Benchmarking

Types of Pay Structures

Overtime Rules

Equity Increases

Compensation for Multiple Generations

Intrinsic/Extrinsic Compensation

Compensation Philosophy

Internal vs. External Equity

Job Evaluation Programs

Market Value of a Position

Pay Compression

Cost of Living Adjustments

Types of Promotion Increases

NOTE: Terms in *red italics* in the following text are defined in the Glossary.

What is base pay?

Base pay is the hourly or annualized salary rate of pay that an employee earns for work performed. It does not include shift premiums, geographical differentials, overtime, or holiday pay.

What is the purpose of a base pay program?

A base pay program provides structure and organizes your jobs so you can attract and retain talent. Also, it often provides career pathing. And finally, it helps to ensure internal and external equity and non-discrimination in compensation.

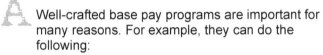

Q **Why is a properly designed base pay program important to my organization?**

A Well-crafted base pay programs are important for many reasons. For example, they can do the following:

- Provide appropriate pay ranges for recruitment
- Promote accurate job descriptions
- Provide a basis for determining the external value of jobs to market
- Provide baselines for reviewing employee performance and rewarding desired behaviors
- Ensure costs are maintained and managed appropriately
- Help reduce turnover through improved employee morale and engagement when pay is not a dissatisfier

Q **What are the elements of a base pay program? Where do I begin?**

A The fundamental elements of a base pay program include the following:

- Compensation philosophy
- Market data guidelines
- Key messages
- Job analysis
- Job documentation
- Job evaluation
- Market data
- Base pay structure

Q **What is the difference between *intrinsic* and *extrinsic* components of compensation?**

A The *intrinsic* part of compensation is the psychological reward an employee gets from doing meaningful work and doing it well. It is a combination of job design and job fulfillment.

The *extrinsic* piece of compensation is both financial (direct and indirect) and non-financial (such as benefits, perks, and other non-financial total rewards elements). It is referred to as extrinsic because it is external to the work itself and others control its size and whether the employee receives it.

Q **What is the direct financial element of compensation?**

A It is comprised of both *fixed* pay elements (base pay and any differential pay such as a shift differential) and *variable* pay elements (such as profit sharing, incentive, bonuses or commissions).

Q **What is the indirect financial element of compensation?**

A Indirect financial compensation is comprised of the protection programs that are mandatory (social security, workers compensation and unemployment) as well as those that are voluntary (pension, medical, dental, and disability). It also includes pay for time not worked. This is further broken down into time not worked *while at the workplace*, such as employee breaks, lunches, and training; and time not worked *while AWAY from the workplace*, such as vacation, holidays, personal days, and sick days or medical leave. And finally, it also includes employee services and perks like discounts, recognition, and company-provided transportation.

Q **What total rewards tools are available to an employee?**

A There are both *quantitative* and *qualitative* total rewards tools. Employers should use as many as possible to attract, retain, and motivate employees. *Quantitative* tools are base pay, benefits, and variable pay. *Qualitative* tools, on the other hand, include career growth and development, workplace culture initiatives, work flexibility options, appreciation and recognition programs, and training and development opportunities.

COMPENSATION: PART ART, PART SCIENCE

Compensation is part science in the way it uses principles, policies and practices to develop effective compensation programs. It is part art in how those principles, policies and practices are applied. Compensation isn't always black and white in how it is designed, implemented, and managed; sometimes you must operate in grey areas when developing and executing compensation programs.

Compensation $ense 101

Q What should my organization consider when it develops a Compensation Philosophy?

A One key consideration for your big-picture *philosophy* is what percent of the benchmarked market pay rate you want to target for your various employee groups. For example, do you want your non-management pay philosophy to be at the 50th percentile, also known as the market average? Likewise, what do you want your management pay philosophy to be? The same 50th percentile, or perhaps higher at the 75th percentile?

Q What are *market data guidelines* and why do I need them?

A *Market data guidelines* are the Compensation Philosophy for each employee group, as well as the scope you will use for *benchmark comparators*. These are typically employee size, industry type, geography, and some financial measure. This financial measure can be revenue size, asset size, or budget size depending on the type of industry you are benchmarking.

Q What is *internal* vs. *external equity*?

A *Internal equity* consists of your job analysis, job documentation, and job evaluation processes. *External equity* is your market pricing process. It is important that internal and external equity are in balance. Sometimes internal equity will override external equity and vice versa, but best practice is to balance the two.

Q What does *Job Analysis* entail?

A *Job Analysis* is a systematic and formal study of job content. It is the process of obtaining important and relevant information about a job.

22

Base Pay

Q **Why would a company perform a Job Analysis?**

A A Job Analysis is important for several reasons. For example, it can provide a solid foundation for the following:

- Work procedure documentation for training purposes
- Performance appraisal standards
- Identification of job families and career paths
- Identification of work performance qualifications
- The legal defense basis for a job's *exemption status*

Q **How is a Job Analysis completed?**

A To complete a Job Analysis, first identify the information to be collected, the sources of that information, and who will collect the data. Next, collect information on the nature and level of work. Some organizations interview people while others use a *Job Content Questionnaire* to gather the information about the job. Finally, use the data collected to evaluate and/or document the job.

Q **What are some sources of job information?**

A There are primary and secondary sources. *Primary* sources include direct observation, individual interviews, diaries/logs, questionnaires, technical consultation, and group interviews. *Secondary* sources include industry association materials, work flow studies, policies and procedures manuals, organization charts, job documentation, survey descriptions, organization goals/objectives, and government publications.

Q **What types of data are important to gather during Job Analysis?**

A When performing a Job Analysis, it is important for most companies to capture data regarding the following:

- Skills
- Tasks
- Experience
- Equipment used
- Job duties
- Job content
- Knowledge required for the position
- Job authority and responsibilities
- Performance standards

Compensation $ense 101

Q **What do I do with the data I gathered in the Job Analysis?**

A Once data gathering is complete, you can use that information to write a job description. Typically, job descriptions contain the following:

- Job title
- FLSA exemption status
- Job department
- Reporting relationships
- General summary of the job (2 to 3 sentences)
- Essential job duties and responsibilities
- Minimum qualifications to perform the job
- Competencies needed for the job
- Working conditions
- A disclaimer statement
- Approval signatures with dates

Job descriptions should be brief, typically 2 to 3 pages each. Job descriptions are not meant to be a procedures manual or performance standards document.

Q **What are some good guidelines to follow for job titles?**

A Job titles should be descriptive of the nature and level of work performed. Avoid inflating titles. However, you should consider internal and external status issues. For example, when determining whether a position should be titled Sales Representative or Business Development Manager, assign the title they need on their business card that best empowers them to do their job.

You don't need to be overly creative with titles. Also, consider any *HRIS* system limitations you might have. Finally, be sure you can easily identify who manages people and who does not.

It is often a good practice, for instance, to put "Manager" *at the end* of the job title if the employee manages people, but to place "Manager" *in front* of the title if they manage a process. An example would be Payroll Manager (manages people) vs. Manager of Payroll (manages payroll processes, policies, and procedures, but does not manage people).

Base Pay

Q: What are the objectives of the last piece of internal equity: *job evaluation*?

A: The objectives of job evaluation are to determine the relative worth of the job to the organization, to identify and correct any pay inequalities, and to facilitate assignment of pay levels for each job.

Q: What types of job evaluation programs are there?

A: There are two types: *non-quantitative* (meaning the evaluation uses no numbers or points and is more descriptive) and *quantitative* (meaning the evaluation uses some type of numbering or point-based system for evaluation).

Q: What are some examples of *non-quantitative* **job evaluation programs?**

A: Ranking, classification, slotting, and job families are typical non-quantitative job evaluation programs. There are pros and cons to each, and some are better than others based on the size of the organization.

Q: What are some examples of *quantitative* **job evaluation programs?**

A: The most commonly used quantitative method is a Point-Factor Rating System. This method determines the relative value of a job based on total points assigned to it. Because a quantitative job evaluation program can be expensive and time consuming to develop and implement in-house, it is usually best to purchase this type of system or have it developed by an outside consultant.

Q: What is *market benchmarking*?

A: *Market benchmarking* is the process of identifying competitive pay levels for jobs in the external market (external equity). It helps companies establish their job worth hierarchy. Also, market benchmarking typically supplements the job evaluation process, although some organizations use pay systems based solely on market benchmarking. Regardless of your type of pay program, market benchmarking is crucial.

25

What are some key things to know about market benchmarking to ensure it is done appropriately?

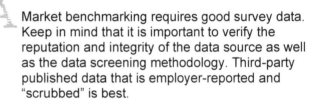

Market benchmarking requires good survey data. Keep in mind that it is important to verify the reputation and integrity of the data source as well as the data screening methodology. Third-party published data that is employer-reported and "scrubbed" is best.

You will use both general industry data (for jobs that can be done across industries) and explicit industry data for industry-specific jobs. Matches should be based on the survey description and not the job title. A good general rule is that a survey match is a good match if it represents 70% or more of your organization's job content. Don't rely on a single source; use at least two different survey sources to give validity to the data. Market benchmark at least 85% of your jobs to build a sound pay structure.

DATA SCRUBBING

Data scrubbing is the process a third party performs to look for "outliers" and question data when it does not align with other reported data.

What are the pitfalls of using free salary data?

With free salary data, the quality you get usually equals the cost: zero! This is because data is typically only reported by job title, and there are no job definitions to help determine a correct position-to-position match. Also, there are usually no data breakouts for experience levels. Rather, all experience is combined into one data point, so you don't get comparative data for 3 years' experience vs. 15 years' experience. And finally, the data is not company-reported by specialists who know how to match jobs. Rather, the data is typically self-reported by employees, and this makes the data entries more subjective and prone to reporting errors.

Q **What can an employer do when an employee claims to be underpaid based on publicly available free survey data?**

A Be prepared to explain in general terms the company's compensation philosophy, as well as which surveys the company gets their comparative market benchmarking data from, and what market data scopes the company uses. If you can be transparent with the employee about their individual salary range and where the employee is positioned in the pay range, it typically will help ease the employees' concerns. Of course, an employer should be sure beforehand that each employee is placed appropriately within the designated pay range.

Q **How do I determine the market value of a position when I cannot get any market benchmarking data for it?**

A There are two methods to use in this situation. First, you can slot the job into your pay structure by simply placing it in a pay grade with other similar internal jobs based on skill, education, effort and responsibility. The second method would be to develop a *market reference group*. In this method, you would pick 4 or 5 other jobs similar to the job for which you need a market benchmarking value. Average the available market value of those jobs and use that market reference group average as the value for the job in question.

Q **Is it important to market benchmark executives too?**

A Yes. Benchmarking of key executive positions can help ensure attraction and retention. There is typically a separate compensation philosophy for executives. This philosophy might deviate from one covering other employees in that executive benchmarking may focus heavily on total cash compensation and pay mix between base and bonus/incentive pay. Whether an organization plans to develop their executives internally or recruit from the external market, it is important to understand the value of each key executive role and where these executives should be paid relative to market based on their education, related experience, and performance. Because organizations invest a lot in developing or recruiting key executives, it is essential to ensure their compensation is competitive.

Compensation $ense 101

 What are my options for a pay structure?

 There are seven different types of pay structures:

- Traditional pay grades
- *Step pay*, or seniority-based pay
- *Skill/knowledge-based pay*
- *Market-based pay*
- *Broadbanding*
- *Competency-based pay*
- *Job family*

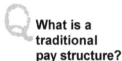 **What is a traditional pay structure?**

 Traditional pay structures typically include enough pay grades to cover all jobs from entry level to executive. A pay grade has a minimum, midpoint and maximum salary for a job. Range widths can span from 40% to 70% from bottom to top. This is a very common pay structure in many organizations.

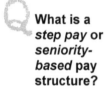 **What is a *step pay* or seniority-based pay structure?**

 With a step pay or seniority-based pay structure, pay adjustments are made based on time-in-job. The pay range is divided into many pay rates with increases related to length of service. These structures are typically used in manufacturing, distribution, or union environments.

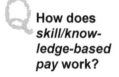 **How does skill/knowledge-based pay work?**

 In a skill/knowledge-based pay structure, pay is specific to the person and not the job. All employees start at the same rate and advance one level for each new job or skill they can perform. It works well if you want to reward pay based on additional skills or knowledge learned. Regular rotation utilizing the job skill or knowledge is important to this type of pay program.

Q **Why do some companies use a *market-based* pay structure?**

A In a market-based pay structure, a pay range is established for each job based on available market benchmarking data. It ignores internal equity and only focuses on external market value. This can create a large volume of work and upkeep. However, a market-based pay structure allows the pay range to be closely tied to the market value of a position; and this enables you to change a particular pay range rather than the ranges for an entire structure.

Q **What is a *broadbanding* pay structure option?**

A A broadbanding pay structure has a career-development focus and is characterized by large groupings of jobs using band criteria. Band criteria might include the types of decision-making the position involves, the type or level of contributions typical for the position, etc. It has few ranges with wide range spreads from 80% to 150%. Broadbanding typically encourages and rewards employees for up, down, and lateral career movement.

While it may seem strange that a career-development focus would reward employees when moving laterally or down in the organization, a broadbanding pay structure recognizes that sometimes this is necessary for subsequent lateral or upward movement. An example might be a scientist going to a different discipline which might be valued less in the organizational hierarchy but broadens skills in preparation for a management role in the scientific area.

Q **Are there good *competency-based pay structures*?**

A A competency-based structure attempts to provide pay based on individual competency levels. It is difficult to determine success rates using this pay structure because market data on competencies is not easily available. However, competency components can often now be found in performance management systems and are loosely tied to merit or used for development purposes only.

Competency-based pay structures are not recommended for most organizations as they are difficult to design, implement and manage. If you believe one is appropriate for your company, consult with a compensation expert to improve the likelihood of success.

Q: And what is the *job family* pay structure based on?

A: The job family pay structure is typically a grouping of similar jobs or functions, such as all management jobs or all finance jobs in a larger organization. There are several levels within a job family determined by skills, knowledge, and experience. A pay range is then developed for each level within a job family.

Q: How do we select the best pay structure for our organization?

A: Consider your business environment (scarcity of labor, unionization, ability to pay vs. the market, and high/low use of incentive pay). Consider also the level of management support you have (budget for staffing and training in compensation, use of outside consultants, commitment to execute final results, and ease of communication). Don't forget to consider the compensation function (size of compensation staff, technical competencies, and availability of labor market data), as well.

Finally, the most important consideration is to evaluate your organizational culture, including the following factors:

- Centralized or decentralized decision making
- Demand for quick re-evaluation of positions
- Level of bureaucracy
- Overall support and trust in the Human Resources (HR) department
- Compensation program communication style (open or closed)
- Preference and emphasis on equity type: internal vs. external

Q: How can we determine our cost of implementation for the pay structure?

A: Once you have your pay ranges created, gather basic data on each employee. This would typically include name, job title, hire date, current annualized rate of pay, etc. Then compare the employee's annualized pay rate to the new pay range.

Employees below the range minimum are considered "green circled" and you will want to move their pay rate to the minimum or above their pay range minimum as soon as is fiscally possible.

Base Pay

Employees above the range maximum are considered "red circled". In this case, most employers either freeze pay until the pay range catches up and the maximum eventually exceeds the annualized pay rate or provide lump sum pay increases. In fact, it is a leading practice to reward employees with a lump sum performance-based increase once they are at or above the maximum of their pay range. This approach continues to reward good performing long-tenured employees without growing the regular base pay rate too far from market.

What is *pay compression*?

Pay compression (the distance of pay between employees) can become less as you hire new employees and perhaps must pay them more due to talent shortages, movement of the market rate, etc. When that happens, review the pay level of current employees in the same job title compared to new employees; and then determine if pay adjustments for current employees should occur to widen the pay gap between them and new employees. Also watch for pay compression between non-exempt employees and their supervisor. If non-exempt employees are getting a lot of overtime, their wages could become very close to their supervisor.

When do I have to pay overtime?

Overtime must be paid to non-exempt employees who do not qualify for a *Fair Labor Standards Act (FLSA)* exemption. All hours those employees work in excess of 40 in a week must be paid at one and one-half times the regular rate.

Are companies still giving general increases or *Cost of Living Adjustments (COLA)*?

Most companies only use these types of increases if they truly cannot measure, or if it is extremely time consuming to measure, individual performance. For example, this might be the case in a manufacturing facility. If you are going to provide *COLA* increases, decide the following:

- If the COLA will be given as a percent of pay or as a flat dollar amount
- Frequency of such increases
- Who will be eligible for these increases
- The basis for the increase (i.e., the Consumer Price Index [CPI], general wage movement, bargaining agreement, or inflation rate)

Compensation $ense 101

 What other types of pay increases typically occur within an organization?

 Other pay increases are normally given for equity reasons, market adjustments, promotions/career development, and merit.

 What are *equity increases* and why would my organization give these increases?

 Equity increases are pay increases given when an employee is not appropriately placed in their pay range based on their education, experience, and performance. Equity increases are sometimes also given when the difference in pay between employees in the same job cannot be justified through education, experience, or performance. *Market adjustments* are also sometimes referred to as equity adjustments. (See the next question on market adjustments.)

To help maintain balance and compensation equity (think parity and fairness) throughout your organization, budget some funds for an annual internal equity review.

What could such a review determine? For starters, it could help you see if internal compensation "compression" is occurring in your organization. The compression of employee salaries can happen over time.

To help ensure compensation equity, you should review the education, experience, and performance of every employee in the same job title. If their pay is not properly aligned, make the necessary – and equitable – corrections.

A *discrimination analysis* might also indicate some equity adjustments are needed.

See additional information in the chapter on *Compliance*

Q **What is a market adjustment?**

A A *market adjustment* occurs when the market pay moves faster than your employee's pay moves with their annual merit increases, and thus the employee's pay falls way behind market.

Periodic market reviews are always a good idea and help you to uncover if you need to make any market adjustments. While overall salary and total compensation averages can sometimes be predictable, big jumps in market data do happen for certain positions. In particular, these jumps may result from market demand for a shallow pool of talent with specific and highly desirable skills. Knowing that certain members of your team are in high demand can help you determine where to make pay adjustments beyond merit increases. This can help you retain key employees and not be blindsided by critical staff departures.

Q **Are there different types of promotion increases?**

A There are generally two types of promotion increases. The first is typically a result of a grade change in a traditional pay structure or a band change in a "broadbanded" structure. This type of increase is generally larger than any other type of increases an employee might receive. To determine if this type of increase is applicable, review the minimum of the new grade or band, what other employees in the same job title are paid, and what the employee being promoted brings to the new job in terms of skills, education, and previous related experience.

The second type of promotional increase is commonly referred to as a *career development increase*. This occurs when an employee has absorbed additional responsibilities that require additional or higher skill sets. This is not a change because of increased volume of work to perform. Rather, this is a smaller change than a promotion. While it would not result in a grade or band change, an employer might want to recognize this change with a smaller increase similar to a merit increase.

What is the purpose of *merit pay*?

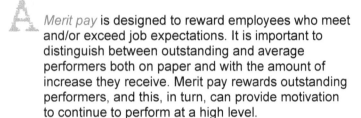

Merit pay is designed to reward employees who meet and/or exceed job expectations. It is important to distinguish between outstanding and average performers both on paper and with the amount of increase they receive. Merit pay rewards outstanding performers, and this, in turn, can provide motivation to continue to perform at a high level.

What are the options for the timing of merit pay delivery?

Most organizations use either an anniversary-based, or focal time-based approach to award merit pay. The *anniversary-based method* spreads the performance review activity out all year if the merit increase is tied to the performance review. While not uncommon, it is much harder to budget for anniversary-based increases.

Focal time-based method is completed within a concentrated effort and time whereby all employees receive their pay increases at the same time in the calendar year. It provides a better comparison of one employee to another and is usually better for staying within budget. Sometimes organizations will have all non-exempt employees on one focal date and all exempt employees on a different date.

What should you consider when choosing a merit pay methodology?

There are many options for awarding merit dollars. It is important to consider the following:

- Merit pool size
- Amount of manager flexibility you will allow in determining merit pay
- Possibly allowing larger increases to those employees low in their range
- Possibly tying (directly or indirectly) the performance appraisal to the increase amount
- What type(s) of communication messages you want to send

Base Pay

Q What are some considerations when distributing low merit budget pools?

A In a tight economy or in a company with a tight budget, many organizations might need to lower their *merit budget* pools. This creates the challenge of how to distribute those dollars from low to high performers. For example, if you have a merit pool of less than 3%, it becomes difficult to distinguish between performers utilizing a grid approach based on both location in pay range and performance rating.

There is, however, a different way to deal with low merit budget pools. One option is to establish the pool of money associated with, for example, a 2% merit budget. Then, rather than a percent awarded for a performance rating, a flat dollar amount could be awarded. If your organization has tracked overall performance ratings for a couple of years, you can then determine your normal distribution pattern. This way, you could model what flat dollar amount for each performance level can be given and still come in on budget. Lump sum dollars look more attractive with a low merit budget than a percent does. Typically, an employee likes to hear they are getting a $1,000 increase as opposed to a 1% increase, even if the amounts are equivalent.

Q What are the pros and cons of providing lump sum increases?

A As stated above, one advantage of a lump sum increase is that, to the employee, dollars are more attractive than percentages. Lump sum payouts are beneficial to the company because the increase is delivered as a one-time occurrence and it saves the company incremental benefit costs when you are not elevating the base pay. It is important, of course, to know how pay is defined for each benefit (by reviewing your plan summary descriptions) so you will know if your organization will save incremental benefit costs on lump sum awards.

The disadvantages to making lump sum awards are that most employees understand their base pay rate is not growing. Also, it is perhaps more likely for employees to resign after a lump sum payout, thus costing the company more money than if that amount had been paid out as an annual percentage increase that is apportioned paycheck-by-paycheck.

Q **What should I think about when establishing my organization's merit pay budget and process?**

A Once you determine your merit pool budget, consider how the organization will fund the merit pool. Where will the money come from and what will be the effect on the business? Will the business have to raise prices, increase margins, or sell more to fund pay increases?

As noted previously, you also need to decide if pay awards will be a percent of pay or a flat dollar amount. If you are doing a percent of pay, what date will base salaries be used for calculation purposes? It is best to freeze base pay increases for 30 to 60 days until merit pay is finalized and awarded. If you are going to use a percent of pay, you might also want to look at the historical average and distribution for the past 2 to 3 years to model what budget number you will need, and how distribution would fit the budget number.

Other things to consider include the following:

- Will you enforce a pre-determined distribution of performance ratings? Or will you allow open distribution wherein there are no set forced percentages of employees who qualify as "Outstanding", "Meets performance standards", "Does not meet performance standards" etc.?
- Will you determine the percentage increase associated with ratings before or after ratings are completed?
- How you will truly reward top performers?

See additional information in the chapter on *Compensation Administration*.

Q **With multiple generations now in the workforce, how do I balance all their pay expectations?**

A With five generations in today's workforce, it can be challenging to manage them fairly and effectively. To address their work life, compensation, and total employee rewards expectations, you must first define their differences and understand their divergent needs.

Traditionalists (also known as "The Silent Generation") are the oldest generation in today's workforce. According to the Pew Research Center, this generation was born during the period from 1928 to 1945.

Traditionalists value loyalty, authority, dedication, sacrifice, honor, and discipline. They are motivated by flexibility, work autonomy, and working on preferred projects. They will often stay on board to bridge a knowledge gap.

Traditionalists typically need creative compensation packages. They crave appreciation, recognition, and work schedule flexibility to spend time with grandchildren. They desire traditional benefit packages, defined benefit retirement plans, and conventional vacation/time off. Certain standard health and insurance benefits are less important if they have Medicare. Traditionalists want coaching focused on improving their strengths.

The *Baby Boomer generation* is comprised of those persons born during the period from 1946 to 1964. Having experienced post-World War II optimism and opportunity, Baby Boomers remain optimistic and engaged. Determined to do better than their parents, they are motivated by money, titles, recognition and respect.

Having invented the 60-hour work week, Baby Boomers go the extra mile. They like status symbols – anything that differentiates them from others, such as a corner office. Internal employee equity is important to them. They desire individual rewards and respond well to coaching focused on improving their weaknesses.

Generation X, defined by Pew as those individuals born during the period from 1965 to 1980, are the offspring of Traditionalists and/or Baby Boomers. They have a chronic need for stimulation and instant gratification. They believe in doing things their way despite the rules – which can potentially raise ethics issues.

Gen X workers are motivated by incentives tied to individual results. They prefer the best office technology over the corner office. They work hard, play hard, and crave work/life balance that includes a flexible schedule. They seek options in tasks, challenges, and new processes; and they want freedom to use their own resourcefulness to achieve success. Gen Xers desire pay increases tied to individual performance, as well as personal rewards for results. They respond well to coaching focused equally on improving strengths and weaknesses.

Millennials (also known as "Generation Y") already comprise the largest group in the labor force. Born during the period from 1981 to the late 1990s, their representation will continue to expand, soon comprising as much as 75% of the global workforce.

Millennials are well-traveled global citizens, and many speak a second language. They desire constant feedback and meaningful work. Surveys show work/life balance is highly valued by as many as 88% of this group.

Millennials like spot awards and non-financial incentives like group outings and travel rewards. They have financial concerns often driven by significant college loan debt. Millennials desire immediate performance feedback; and they want not only to hear how *you* feel they are doing, but to share how *they* feel they are doing. Millennials want at least one touch point per week from their direct manager. They respond to coaching focused primarily on their weaknesses. And they will leave an organization devoid of performance improvement or leadership development opportunities.

Overlapping with the final birth years of the Millennials, *Generation Z* (also known as "The iGeneration") workers are the youngest in today's workforce. This is the most diverse generation and many Gen Z workers are bilingual/multilingual. Digital natives with short attention spans, they are eager to work, motivated by job security, and want to contribute to meaningful work.

Gen Z members focus on personal development and opportunities for advancement. This is the first generation in decades open to skipping college and going directly into the workforce if it provides education in their field of interest. They respond to teaching-oriented coaching. Honesty, good communication, and a solid vision are the most important leadership qualities to Generation Z employees.

Q **So, how can our company balance the total rewards expectations of these diverse generations?**

A Above all, create uniquely focused experiences that engage and empower diverse individuals to achieve a shared strategic vision and business objectives. Beyond this, do the following:

- Communicate uniquely with each generation as they prefer
- Accommodate employee differences in coaching
- Offer workplace choices in compensation and benefits
- Provide flexible, adaptive leadership
- Respect and reward competence and initiative
- Take necessary steps to enhance employee satisfaction and loyalty

Build and promote a learning environment to attract and retain diverse individuals

Q **How do I keep my compensation programs updated?**

A Because market and organizational conditions are constantly changing, make it a priority to regularly review and determine if your programs are effective, efficient, and appropriate. Ensure your pay program is being administered according to standard employer policies and procedures. Determine if your pay program is strong enough to withstand the risk of challenge from employees, government agencies, and other third parties. And finally, ensure there is an understanding of roles and responsibilities between HR and line managers for administering the plan. A *Manager's Compensation Guide* can help with documenting and aligning roles and responsibilities.

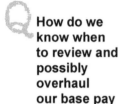

Q **How do we know when to review and possibly overhaul our base pay program?**

A If your base pay system has been in place for 3 years or longer, it is almost certainly time for a fresh look. And if your base pay system has been in place for 5 years or more, chances are pretty good it has fallen behind competitive standards in the marketplace. If that's the case, your company could be paying too much for your staff talent, paying too little to attract new hires, or simply be focusing on the wrong types of compensation that matter in your industry.

If you established your current pay and compensation programs 3 years ago, 5 years ago, or even longer, you should have been frequently monitoring industry standards and benchmarks and making any necessary adjustments. If your compensation systems have simply been static, however, with no real competitive monitoring or corrections, your organization may be seriously out of sync with your industry. That can hurt your company in terms of its financial position, employee retention, and job candidate appeal. On the other hand, if your base pay system has been maintained prudently, and you are benchmarking your roles every couple of years, and moving your ranges at least that often, your organization's base pay program is probably in good shape.

Q **How often should we adjust our pay structure?**

A Typically, pay structures should be adjusted annually or bi-annually. This timing decision should be made in relation to the merit budget decision. Do not move your salary structure at the same pace as your overall merit budget, as this limits an employees' opportunity to move through their pay range.

Pay Differentials

In this section you will learn about...

Geographic Differentials   Market Data

Shift Premiums   Hazard Pay

NOTE: Terms in *red italics* in the following text are defined in the Glossary.

What are *pay differentials*?

Pay differentials are those conditions for which an employer is willing to compensate an employee with additional pay.

Why do pay differentials matter?

Pay differentials are typically used to entice employees to take certain assignments or work under less desirable conditions. For example, pay differentials might be used to encourage employees to work hard-to-staff shifts such as second or third shift. Pay differentials might also be used to get employees to work in hazardous conditions, or to influence employees to take jobs in geographical areas with a higher *cost of living*.

If I have employees in multiple locations across states, do I need *geographic* differentials?

It is certainly wise to determine both the "*cost of salary*" and the "cost of living" for each city and state where your employees work. When differences between these two costs are +/- 5%, it is common to create a geographic pay differential. Overall, the number of geographic pay differentials created may depend upon how tight your company needs to manage its salary line. For example, to keep your number of pay differentials low, you might establish a 7.5% pay range increase for those differentials between 5 to 10%. (The 7.5% increase is the average of the 5 to 10% range.) Likewise, a 13.5% pay range increase could be established where differentials of 11 to 15% are used.

If I use national *market data*, do I still need geographic differentials?

Yes, even if you use national *market data*, you will still need geographic differentials for both high and low cost-of-salary or cost-of-living variances. Utilizing different salary ranges based on geographic differentials also makes it easier to conduct *internal equity reviews* or *discrimination analyses*.

Couldn't I establish geographical differentials based on regions in the U.S.?

Yes, you could establish your geographic differentials this way. However, if you are going to utilize this method, contact a reliable third-party survey resource to get appropriate information for each region (such as Midwest or Northeast, etc.). It will be important to know how much higher or lower each region is compared to National data; or how much higher or lower each region is when compared with your primary headquarters location. Be aware, however, that this methodology does not recognize big swings in cost of salary or cost of living within a region. You may find you need higher geographic differentials in some areas within a region because the regional approach is, by its nature, high-level and general.

Should we lump geographic differentials in with other base pay?

It is always best to make geographic differentials a separate line item on the employee's paycheck. This way, if an employee changes jobs to work in a location with a different geographic pay differential (or no geographic differential at all), it is easier to change or eliminate the differential. Ultimately, that will ease communication with the employee about the change.

Q **What is a *shift premium* and how does it typically work?**

A *Shift premium* is an additional premium paid to entice employees to work a shift considered a hardship. A shift premium is typically paid for second- or third-shift hours. (Each organization defines what hours constitute each shift.) A shift premium is typically paid as additional cents per hour or as an additional percentage of pay. Third-shift premium is typically a higher amount than second shift premium. As with geographic pay differentials, it is always best to put any shift premium pay differential on a separate line on the employee's paycheck; this is helpful if the employee changes work shifts and the shift premium needs to be adjusted or eliminated.

Q **How is an employee who works part of a second and part of a third shift typically paid shift premium?**

A Second-shift hours are usually paid at the second shift premium rate and third-shift hours are paid at the third-shift premium rate. Alternatively, some employers opt to pay the shift premium associated with the shift where the most hours are worked.

Q **What is *hazard pay*?**

A *Hazard pay* is a premium differential paid to employees in recognition of difficult and hazardous working conditions. The hazard pay differential is offered as an incentive to motivate employees to work in hazardous occupations.

Incentive Plans

In this section you will learn about...

Short- and Long-Term Plans

Manufacturing/Production Plans

Team Plans

Customer Contact Plans

Optimum Plan Payout Frequency

Goal and Gain Sharing Plans

Management Plans

Sales Compensation Plans

Payout Levels and Amounts

Funding an Incentive Plan

NOTE: Terms in *red italics* in the following text are defined in the Glossary.

Q **What are *incentive plans*?**

A Incentive plans are variable pay that must be re-earned by hitting goals and objectives during a given period, typically quarterly or annually. Due to the reality of periodic and inevitable economic downturns, employers have been increasingly implementing variable pay incentive plans while putting less money and emphasis on *merit pay*.

Q **Why are incentive plans important?**

A Incentive plans, if appropriately designed, can help drive job performance, behaviors and results needed to achieve business objectives. Additionally, if incentive plan goals are tied closely to objectives an individual can truly influence, these goals can keep employees engaged and motivated to deliver better bottom line results.

Q **What are some types of incentive plans?**

A There are both short-term and long-term incentive plans. The most frequent *short-term incentive plans* include goal sharing or gain sharing (which are company-wide plans), as well as *Manufacturing or Production Plans*, *Management Plans*, *Team Plans*, *Sales Compensation Plans*, and *Customer Contact Plans*.

47

continued

Long-term incentive plans are usually in place for three to five years and are typically designed for senior management or very high-level individual contributors who can strategically and significantly drive business results. Long-term incentive reward programs typically include *Stock Plans* and *Cash Plans*. Stock Plans feature awards in the form of company stock which vests at a certain percentage each year. Cash Plans, on the other hand, might start out with a lower cash payout in the first year, and then escalate to the largest cash payout in the final plan year.

What are *goal sharing* and *gain sharing* plans, and how do they work?

A *Goal Sharing Incentive Plan* focuses on business unit performance while rewarding participants for achieving continuous improvement results. This type of program typically takes a *balanced scorecard* approach with goals to improve processes, financial performance, quality, customer satisfaction, and growth.

A *Gain Sharing Incentive Plan* shares rewards based on financial gain only. Typically, only financial metrics are included to define successful achievement of the gain sharing objective. While this is considered a short-term plan because it is applied within the context of a fiscal reporting year, a Gain Sharing Plan can typically remain in place for many years once implemented.

Goal Sharing Plans and Gain Sharing Plans are most frequently paid annually. Because of this, and based on repeated achievement of the plan objectives, they can quickly become an expectation to receive a payout every year. Thus, the first year a plan does not pay out can create communication challenges, but also presents an opportunity to remind employees and reinforce the fact that the plan is *variable pay*. Variable pay is *at-risk* pay.

Q **What are Manufacturing/ Production Incentive Plans?**

A These plans are typically designed only for employees who work in a manufacturing or production area. Measurement criteria for Manufacturing/Production Incentive Plans might include quality, productivity, cost containment, and some type of customer service metric. Measurements are typically based on what manufacturing and production employees can truly impact, with results posted monthly.

These plans usually pay monthly or quarterly depending on the level of dollars an employee can earn and how frequently a company wants to reinforce the behavior desired. Naturally, these plans typically pay more as results increase and less as results decrease depending on the measures designed and results needed.

Q **Are *Management Plans* designed only for employees who manage others?**

A Management Plans are designed for management employees as well as certain high-level individual contributors. This type of plan includes financial parameters and individual objectives. It may also include leadership objectives or other discretionary components. The weighting percentage assigned to discretionary components should be kept low.

Those employees covered under a management plan are usually eligible for a percentage of pay reward based on their level in the organization. It is important to be careful designing rewards that are a percentage of pay because salary increases automatically increase the bonus amount.

Management Plans are usually based on achieving annual goals and are, therefore, most often paid annually. It is important that individual objectives are designed as *"stretch goals"* and are reviewed by two layers of management to ensure an appropriate amount of *stretch* has been set for the measurement.

How are
Team Plans
typically
used?

 Team Plans encourage employees to work together to achieve results. These plans can be effective for organizations that want to drive continuous improvement and empower teams to truly drive their results. At a minimum, Team Plans normally have some form of productivity, quality, cost, and customer service measurements. They are often very similar to production-type plans. Team Plans can be somewhat self-policing, in that teams will often pressure or weed out those not contributing their fair-share to the results.

 **Are *Sales***
Compensa-
tion Plans
only for
direct sales
employees?

Sales Compensation Plans, naturally, are typically designed for sales-focused employees. They can include incentives for direct sales personnel, as well as inside sales staff and technical consultants supporting direct sales employees. Sales Compensation Plans align very closely with sales performance results, and typically include goals for customer retention, customer growth, profitability, sales growth, and specific product- or service-based sales objectives.

See additional information in the chapter on
Sales Compensation.

 **What is a**
Customer
Contact Plan?

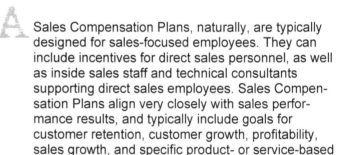 A Customer Contact Incentive Plan commonly applies to staff in corporate call centers. Such a plan can encourage efficient call handling, as well as quality results, call availability time, etc. This type of plan usually pays on results monthly. Sometimes, however, the cost to administer a customer contact incentive plan outweighs the dollars paid for results. Most companies implement Customer Contact Plans if this practice is prevalent in their industry and used by most or all their competitors.

Q **What are the main challenges in designing incentive plans?**

A Primary challenges for incentive plan design include being able to accurately forecast company performance while setting goals at the right level to motivate employees to achieve desired results. It is more difficult to set goals in long-term plans than short-term plans.

Q **What are key parameters for a successful employee incentive compensation plan?**

A No matter which types of employee incentive compensation programs you implement to elevate staff and corporate performance, there are certain key parameters you'll need to establish. For instance, you'll need to determine which employees are eligible for participation and how their rewards will be measured. You'll also need to identify and define plan goals, *weighting factors (or weights)*, payout levels and amounts, reward payout frequency, and funding.

Q **What should you consider when determining which employees are eligible for an incentive program?**

A There are two primary criteria to consider:

1. Eligibility by job category or job classification (e.g., all employees, full-time only, part-timers, temporary staff, etc.)

2. When each type of employee becomes eligible to participate in the incentive program. This may involve rules for factoring in when new employees can receive their first payout, as well as when those leaving or retiring from the organization receive their final payouts. You should also define whether payouts for partial-year participants are pro-rated.

Q **How should our company's employee incentive plan be measured to determine success and payouts?**

A To make the plan understandable and manageable, focus on 3 to 5 measures directly aligned with – and tied to – key performance priorities. Measurement metrics should balance overall company performance with individual contributions toward that performance.

How do we effectively set goals for an incentive plan?

Goals must be clearly established and communicated for employees to understand and strive to achieve them. Goals should be realistic but encourage employees to stretch and "raise the bar". There should be a clear link between performance and pay. Also, the payout should be large enough to justify the effort required to achieve goals.

You will want to develop *SMART goals*. SMART goals are typically defined as:

S = Specific:
Goals should target specific areas for improvement.

M = Measurable:
Goals should be quantifiable or at least suggest an indicator of progress.

A = Achievable:
Goals should be ambitious but within reach with the right amount of effort.

R = Realistic:
Goals should state what results can realistically be achieved given available resources.

T = Time-related:
Goals should specify when results can and should be achieved.

To accurately assess performance relative to these goals, you'll need to establish performance levels such as threshold, target, and maximum. *Threshold performance levels*, for example, should be attainable 80 to 90% of the time, while target levels should be attainable 50 to 60% of the time, and maximum performance goal attainment should be reached 10 to 20% of the time. While the level of payout awarded to performers at each of these levels can be difficult to calculate, the threshold is typically set at 80 to 90% of target performance with maximum at 110 to 120%.

If goals are not appropriate, there can be negative consequences. If goals are set too high, employees will not be motivated because they believe there is little chance of achieving the goals. If the goals are too easy and employees are consistently and easily achieving them, the wrong message is sent that superior performance is not necessary to receive a payout.

Q Should all weights be equally established for all plan measures?

A Employee performance factors and corresponding measures are not created equal. Your plan should weight the most important parameters or business priorities accordingly. For example, during one year, overall business growth might be most important, while the next year the most critical goal might be profitability, cost containment, or customer satisfaction. Weighting communicates priorities and direction, and reflects the desired result for the plan component.

Your plan should seek to balance team and/or individual weights where appropriate. (This can be especially important in customer contact and sales compensation plans.) But keep in mind that multiple goals weighted within a parameter will only serve to diminish the effect of the weighting. Also, no individual parameter should be weighted at less than 10%. As an example, financials might carry a weighting of 60%, an Individual MBO at 20%, a second Individual MBO at 10%, and a third Individual MBO at 10%.

Q What should I consider when establishing payout levels and amounts?

A You will need to determine how each incentive component will pay out. There can be many types of plan payout designs. You could, for instance, pay a flat dollar amount for certain parameters, or a flat percentage of the plan or salary for others. Or you could establish a payout table that pays a lower amount until you are closer to 100% of goal and then pays a lot more when you exceed 100% of that goal. Also, you will need to determine if you want to cap any payouts. Caps are a point at which you want payouts to end.

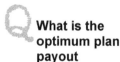

Q **What is the optimum plan payout frequency?**

A When determining optimum plan payout timing, keep in mind that your reward cycles should align with your business cycles and/or your overall plan purpose. You should also consider whether the payout amount earned in the identified time frame will sufficiently motivate the employee.

How often you pay incentive rewards could, of course, depend on the type of plan. For example, Gain Sharing or Goal Sharing Plans, as well as Management Bonus Plans, typically pay annually. Customer Contact Plans or Manufacturing/Production Plans normally pay quarterly or monthly. Sales Compensation Plans usually pay quarterly or monthly depending on whether the plan is an incentive plan or a commission plan. You can also pay different parameters at different times; for instance, you could have a plan with both monthly and quarterly payout parameters.

Q **What is the best method-ology to determine how to fund an incentive plan?**

A For Goal Sharing plans, your company will want to determine how much it wants to share in the form of an incentive payment for achieving continuous improvement results. In other words, how much are you willing to pay for achieving goals to improve processes, financial performance, quality, customer satisfaction, growth, or whatever is on your balanced scorecard.

A Gain Sharing plan, on the other hand, should pay for itself, as it is typically funded through corporate financial growth. Nonetheless, you will still need to determine the level of reward per eligible employee. Once you establish the financial goal for the year, any additional financial attainment above goal could be used to fund a payout. For example, if 110% of the established financial goal is met, you might be willing to share a portion of that additional profit earned with employees. Perhaps employees would get a payout of 3% of their salary if the organization exceeds its financial goals by 10%.

Always model your plans to ensure that sufficient funding is available. It is essential to understand upfront the likely total plan cost and be prepared to fund incentives at all levels of performance. Never assume that plan goals will not be fully realized; and never implement a plan that cannot be fully funded if plan maximums are achieved. By modeling various levels of performance, you can also determine the minimum level of financial performance needed to begin funding the plan.

Is incentive plan design and management complex?

Employee incentive program design and management can, indeed, be complex. It can also be a moving target that necessitates plan changes from one year to the next. But understanding the essential parameters can help you stay on solid ground for rewarding employees as they contribute to your company's success.

Designed, implemented and administered correctly, incentive plan parameters can inspire performance excellence, company loyalty, and healthier corporate profitability. Poorly crafted plans, however, can lead to discouragement, dissention, and costly employee turnover. If you do not have experience in confidently designing incentive plans, hire a compensation consultant to help you design your plans.

Should we have a plan document for our incentive plans?

Every incentive plan should have a plan document that covers eligibility, plan objectives, how attaining the incentive is determined, payout calculations and frequency, as well as terms and conditions (including termination and pro-rated payments among other considerations). You will want to think proactively about all the terms and conditions you might encounter and need, and then document them in your plan. Of course, it is then vitally important to share your plan document with participants.

See additional information in the chapter on *Communicating About Compensation*.

Should we review our incentive plans annually?

 Absolutely! For your incentive plans to be current and relevant, you should measure, review, update and repeat each year. Use the "voice of the customer" (feedback from those who participated in the plan), as well as surveys and metrics to review what went well and what needs corrected or fine-tuned. Then, build an annual formal process to review and update plans including plan documentation.

 How should we ensure incentives are well-designed and productive?

Your employee incentive plans will likely influence your business at three levels: corporate, sales, and departmental. Because sales and departmental performance roll up into the overall corporate impact, incentives at those levels must be well-designed and productive. To evaluate your incentive program design and its success, analyze it from three perspectives:

- Personal Performance: Is the program encouraging and producing desired employee behaviors and results?
- Financial: How is the program affecting the bottom line, and what are the costs?
- Differentiation: Are your top performers also your top incentive earners?

Often, the introduction of an incentive plan can spark improved employee productivity. Unfortunately, this excitement and energy – as demonstrated by improved personal performance – can be short-lived. Continuing communication to remind employees of their incentives, benchmarks and progress in meeting performance goals can certainly help keep them motivated. To make sure this happens:

- Measure employee productivity before, during and after incentive plan cycles. Did the plan drive the desired behaviors? Analyze (or simply observe) performance at various times to make sure.
- If your plan has *MBOs (Management by Objectives)*, analyze incremental and individual results to determine if these objectives were set too low or too high. Remember that unattainable objectives can be de-motivators.
- Conduct employee focus group sessions to find out what they think is (or is not) working, and if the incentive program meets their needs and expectations.

How can we judge the success of an incentive plan?

Behavior, attitudes and productivity all impact the bottom line. To make sure your employee incentive program helps boost financial performance and profitability:

- Measure financial performance before, during and after incentive program cycles. Based on the numbers, can you clearly see whether your incentive program is delivering the expected return on investment? Keep in mind that many factors can impact short-term financial performance, including market factors beyond your control; so, don't make knee-jerk changes to your plan unless those changes are clearly necessary to correct a plan deficiency.
- Zero in on key financial performance metrics. How did your program pay relative to sales or earnings? Did your company have low performance earnings yet pay high on incentive plan results? If the macro or big-picture view of *reward-to-performance ratio* seems off, consider making changes to the program.
- Look at results by department. Are individual team payouts in alignment with the performance of larger organizational units? If this micro view of reward-to-performance indicates problem areas, make sure that any overall program changes benefit the entire company.
- Compare your incentive program payouts to other companies in your market. Be aware that if your plan is far below those of key competitors, you could lose top performers.

Q How can we determine if top performers are also our top incentive earners?

A If everyone seems to get a *"bonus"* regardless of performance, your plan could be a de-motivator to your superstars. To make sure your incentive program rewards excellence, analyze how many employees earned below target, at target and above target. Based on this information, assess whether the targets were realistic in the first place. A good rule-of-thumb is that 10 to 20% should be rewarded at the top level, 60 to 80% should be rewarded less and in the mid-range, and 10 to 20% should be rewarded considerably less (or nothing) for sub-par performance.

Sales Compensation

In this section you will learn about...

Establishing Pay Level Targets

Upside Potential

Sales Compensation Mechanics

Sales Compensation for New Hires

Establishing Pay Mix Balance

Sales Compensation Components

Evaluating Sales Compensation

NOTE: Terms in red italics in the following text are defined in the Glossary.

Q What is sales compensation?

A Sales compensation is typically designed for those employees either in a direct sales role or sometimes a supporting sales role. It is the base pay they receive, as well as the variable pay they receive in the form of a bonus, incentive, or commission for sales they close. There are many factors to consider when designing a sales compensation plan, so read on!

Q Why does sales compensation matter?

A The salesperson has a unique place in the organization. If the salesperson does not feel motivated to perform at a high level, revenues falter. And if sales performance remains at a low level for very long, the organization could fail, leaving dozens or hundreds or even thousands of employees out of work. So, a lot rides on the salesperson feeling satisfied and well-compensated. Of course, because the salesperson's role in the organization is unique, salesperson compensation does not – and usually should not – fit neatly into a compensation structure that might be appropriate for the rest of the organization. Because of the salesperson's role, their working environment and expectations are different from other employees. Thus, it is vital to view their compensation through a different lens, giving due consideration to the role of the salesperson, pay level targets, pay mix and upside potential, components and weightings, the mechanics of the salesperson compensation program, and how to implement and communicate the plan.

Q **Where do I get started designing a Sales Compensation Plan?**

A It is important to first understand that the salesperson's duties are one-of-a-kind in the organization. Because of this, it is easy for the role of the salesperson to be misunderstood, underappreciated and incorrectly compensated. To get a handle on the most appropriate salesperson compensation system, it is critical to be able to answer these questions:

- How are sales team jobs defined in your organization?
- What role do these jobs play in the overall sales process?
- What types of customers do salespersons interact with, and what skill sets are required to perform well with these customers?
- What is the job's primary sales strategy?
- Do salespersons get help from others in the organization, or do they sell on their own?
- What are the products or services being sold?
- Who in the organization is eligible for inclusion in the salesperson's unique compensation plans?

Some of these questions might seem odd when considering the design of an internal compensation system, but identifying the salesperson's operating environment and challenges can be the first crucial step toward appropriate compensation design.

Q **How do I establish pay level targets?**

A It can be more challenging to establish pay level targets for salespersons because their job is so closely aligned with quantifiable performance and the achievement of bottom-line goals. Baseline pay for salespersons is usually accompanied by an incentive or performance-based component such as *commission* for sales. While many, if not most, non-executive jobs in the organization can be assigned a pay level range with increases compared to prior year compensation, the salesperson's compensation program can get more complicated. To adequately assign pay targets, you should consider these and other key factors:

- The organization's sales compensation philosophy
- Good market data about benchmarked jobs in the industry, geographic area, etc.
- Pay structure based on competitive data
- Possible levels of *base pay* vs. *incentive pay*
- The relationship between pay and performance expectations
- Whether the salesperson's activities can be classified more as "hunter" or "farmer"
- The *total target cash* allocated to compensate members of the sales department
- Cost of sales compared to revenue

Q How do I establish balance in the pay mix?

A Traditionally, the salesperson's compensation is a mix of *fixed* (or base) pay and *variable* (at-risk or incentive) pay. Usually, your market (including your industry and location) will dictate what is appropriate. Thus, to be competitive in *attracting* and *retaining* sales talent, your compensation mix should be market-appropriate. In other words, if your sales compensation leans too heavily on commission, you might have trouble retaining sales performers if commissions are not a rewarding and motivating part of their compensation.

You can establish a *Target Mix* of, say, half fixed and half variable pay. This is the amount you forecast as being the likely payout based on performance expectations and budget. Your *Actual Mix,* however, will likely vary somewhat once performance results are in for a given period. Your 50/50 Target Mix, based on $50,000 base pay and $50,000 in commission pay, might end up as an Actual Mix of 56/44 if the base of $50,000 is augmented by only $40,000 in incentive pay.

continued

How can you decide how much emphasis to place on each part of the mix? Again, it can depend on your market, but here are some rules-of-thumb:

Place a heavier emphasis on *base pay* if:

- Sales is more of a team effort
- Heavy use of advertising and promotion means that little sales effort is required (in other words, if market awareness is so high that the salesperson is more of an order-taker than a persuader)

Place a heavier emphasis on *incentive pay* if:

- The sales role requires a high level of skill and drive
- The company is not well-known
- Competition is strong
- The market opportunity is high

Q Why should we focus on total cash compensation with salespersons?

A You want to focus on total cash compensation (base and annual incentive, bonus or commissions) with salesperson compensation because your organization might choose to have more base than bonus pay relative to the market or vice versa. What matters is that your total cash compensation is competitive with market benchmarking of total cash compensation. Each organization decides its pay mix (base pay to incentive ratio) and may choose a pay mix that differs from market norms but must ultimately ensure competitiveness from a total cash compensation perspective.

Q How do we determine appropriate *upside potential*?

A Simply put, if the total plan pay target is $10,000 but the salesperson could earn another $10,000 on top of that, the *upside potential* is 1:1. If the target is $10,000 but the salesperson could earn an additional $20,000 over target, the upside potential is 2:1. Keep in mind how much upside potential the salesperson could earn and how many salespeople might actually be able to achieve that level of results when setting your upside potential.

Sales Compensation

Q **What key components are typically in the design of a Sales Compensation Plan?**

A Components to consider can fall into categories that include:

- Financial or production
- Strategic
- Input or activity
- Subjective or judgment-based

Financial components typically focus on sales dollars, margin or margin dollars, or units. These are mostly measured in volume. *Strategic* components focus on specific customers or products, or on measures that drive a strategic priority. *Activity* components focus on a Sales Representative's specific activities, events or milestones. And *subjective* or *judgment-based* components should normally be less prominent (and carry less weight) because they relate to observational objectives that have less quantifiable results.

When determining which components to include to appropriately reward the salesperson, limit the total number to five or fewer, and do not include any that you would weight at less than 10%. In addition, each included component should be:

- *Controllable* by the salesperson, with the link between sales performance behavior and results clearly relatable and understood
- *Measurable* with metrics that will drive appropriate behavior and that, for higher incentive pay mixes, have a clear "line of sight" to the outcome
- *Aligned* clearly between the business strategy and overall corporate performance

In general, whatever weighting factor (as a percentage) you give a component, make sure it reflects and supports corporate priorities and direction as well as the desired results for the component. If a component is an aggregate corporate number toward which the sales representative's performance has little input or effect, it should be given lighter weight than direct impact sales performance components.

65

What are the important mechanics for a Sales Compensation Plan, and how do we get them right?

Mechanics involve the types of plans such as Commission Plans or Quota Plans, as well as links, bonus multipliers, caps, thresholds, and payout frequency. When setting performance expectations and rewarding performance excellence, consider whether commission plans or quota plans – or some mix of the two – are appropriate.

Commission Plans are typically clear and straightforward, so Sales Representatives find them easy to understand: sell at a certain level and receive a predetermined commission (usually in addition to base pay). Organizations may use varying commission rates for different products; however, commission plans normally pay from the first dollar sold, and the salesperson does not have to reach a threshold level of sales performance to begin earning the commission.

A *Quota Plan,* on the other hand, can help keep the Sales Representative focused on the entire sales process – from booking the sale to shipping and ensuring customer payment. Accurate quota setting can be challenging, so quota plans are most commonly used by companies with a history of sales performance and market analysis over time.

To fine tune your Sales Compensation Plan, you might also consider factoring in links, a bonus multiplier, caps and a threshold. Another important consideration is the frequency of plan payouts.

Links

Some plans link overall company performance components to salesperson compensation. These links are often based on profit and/or revenue. Typically, however, a Sales Representative cannot earn any over-target payout on the revenue measure unless and until they also exceed the target on the profit measure.

66

Bonus Multiplier

If a Sales Representative achieves exceptional results over an assigned goal (for example, if the Representative hits 110% of the annual target by the end of the third quarter), many companies will include a bonus multiplier. This could result in the Representative receiving either a lump sum bonus once the milestone is reached or a bigger payout at the time of the planned payment.

Caps

Some companies may place a cap on plans in which the Representative cannot earn above a certain level. A cap might be appropriate for some measures but not others. For those components that are capped, if the salesperson's compensation hits the cap cycle after cycle, this could be an indication that certain plan elements are not properly structured relative to likely performance attainment.

Threshold

It is often appropriate for a company to set certain minimum performance levels before the salesperson can start earning incentive compensation in a quota-based plan. If it is a commission-based plan, however, this is often accounted for in the base salary.

Payout Frequency

Frequency of compensation program payouts will vary from plan to plan depending on many factors. While the most common frequency is quarterly, the nature of the industry and the marketplace, as well as internal accounting issues, may affect compensation payout frequency. You should also consider how often you can measure and obtain accurate results. Commission plans typically pay monthly while quota plans typically pay quarterly.

What are best practices for implementing and communicating sales compensation plans?

See the chapter on *Communicating About Compensation*.

How should we evaluate the sales compensation program and plan for the next cycle?

It is important to periodically evaluate your Sales Compensation Plan to determine if it is having the intended positive impact on your sales organization and corporate sales results. This can be especially critical if substantial changes to the plan were introduced or market factors have made the status quo of an existing plan questionable. There are three primary ways (or views) to help you determine the effectiveness of your Sales Compensation Plan: *financial, performance,* and *differentiation.*

Financial

Taking a financial view, you can determine how the plan is functioning as well as its costs. This can help you bring into perspective the plan's impact on sales-force earnings along with the company's return on investment from the plan.

Performance

From the performance viewpoint, you can determine if the plan is driving the right behaviors as planned. By analyzing both macro and micro performance factors, you can make large adjustments or do smaller fine tuning as appropriate. Be careful, however, to understand that making large changes based on short measurement periods could cause additional problems. It is generally better to view performance factors as trends in the context of at least a few performance cycles before making large-scale or wholesale changes.

Differentiation

Differentiation can help you determine if top earners are also truly your top performers. Be sure to build into your measurement criteria the necessary performance differentiation data to make this assessment.

Q Should I have a different Sales Compensation Plan for a new hire or simply guarantee their bonus for a specific period?

A There are pros and cons to both approaches. A separate plan for a new hire can be established to drive behaviors that will ultimately set the salesperson up to be successful. The separate plan might include:

- Completing product and service training
- Requiring successfully passing a test to prove knowledge level
- Building the sales plan for their territory
- Building the first plan of pipeline prospects
- Demonstrating a sales customer presentation to a team at the company

The *pro* here is having the Sales Representative complete activities that should successfully set them up to drive sales. The *con* is that you are paying for activities and not results.

The pro to simply guaranteeing bonus payments to a new hire is the security it provides the Sales Representative until they get their feet on the ground; while the con is that you are not guaranteed results, nor are activities being measured which should lead to results.

If you choose to use a different compensation plan for new hires, do not extend the period of the new hire plan for too long. If your salesperson should be able to generate sales within 90 days, do not pay on a new hire plan or guarantee sales bonus payments beyond that period.

Compliance

In this section you will learn about...

Fair Labor Standards Act

Title VII of the Civil Rights Act

Consumer Credit Protection Act

Lilly Ledbetter Fair Pay Act

Department of Labor Audits

Internal Equity Analysis

Family and Medical Leave Act

Equal Pay Act

Age Discrimination Act

Americans with Disabilities Act

Compensation Audits

OFCCP Audits

Discrimination Analysis

NOTE: Terms in *red italics* in the following text are defined in the Glossary.

Q **What is compliance?**

A Compensation compliance is about adhering to all pertinent laws, both federal and state, that govern compensation administration and discrimination.

Q **Why does compliance matter?**

A Compliance with compensation regulations will put you in the best possible position to avoid discrimination and lawsuits; and to be a company where people want to work. Back pay, fines, and other charges can often be devastating to an employer and take funds needed for other areas of the business.

Q **What laws affect compensation?**

A There are many laws – including local, state and federal regulations – that impact how a company designs, implements and administers its compensation and total rewards programs. These include (but are not necessarily limited to) the following:

continued

71

- *Fair Labor Standard Act*
- *Equal Pay Act*
- *Title VII of the Civil Rights Act*
- *Age Discrimination Act*
- *Consumer Credit Protection Act*
- *Americans with Disabilities Act*
- *Lilly Ledbetter Fair Pay Act*

These regulations have been drafted and crafted, debated and mandated over many decades reaching back into our country's past, these worker protection laws are a complex and tangled web. The *Fair Labor Standards Act* is, perhaps, the granddaddy of them all, first enacted in 1938 during the Franklin Roosevelt administration as the Great Depression continued to affect the livelihoods of workers. The 1960s and the Johnson administration brought another wave of worker protection regulations: *The Equal Pay Act* in 1963, *Title VII of the Civil Rights Act* in 1964, the *Age Discrimination Act* in 1967, and the *Consumer Credit Protection Act* concerning wage garnishment in 1968. Since then, two more landmark regulations have entered the corporate compliance landscape: the *Americans with Disabilities Act* in 1992 and the *Lilly Ledbetter Fair Pay Act* in 2009.

It can be daunting to walk safely through this regulatory minefield, so let's take a brief look at each of these regulations.

What does the *Fair Labor Standards Act* entail?

Also known as the *FLSA*, this was the earliest regulation to affect pay, originating in 1938 and amended several times since. This law impacts direct compensation and has many provisions that cover such things as exemptions, minimum wage, overtime child labor restrictions, and recordkeeping requirements.

The *FLSA* is enforced by the Wage and Hour Division of the Department of Labor (or DOL). If you are audited and found to have misclassified employees for exemption purposes, the standard regulatory penalty is two years' back pay to each employee who was in the position during that time. That is for a violation deemed to be non-willful. The penalty increases to three years' back pay for a violation determined to have been willful. What's more, in addition to financial penalties, your company could be prosecuted criminally. To learn more, order the *Handy Reference Guide to the Fair Labor Standards Act* from the Department of Labor.

To avoid *FLSA* noncompliance, it is wise to audit your roles and document which exemption classification each employee qualifies for, and why. Review the exemption classification for each role every time the job description is updated, or when changes occur that affect the role. Also, it is important to contact a labor law attorney anytime you are going to change an employee's exemption status from exempt to non-exempt; that will help you carefully plan that change to lessen any potential employee legal action or morale issues.

Handy Guide to the Fair Labor Standards Act

Obtain your copy of the *Handy Reference Guide to the Fair Labor Standards Act* via this link: **https://www.dol.gov/whd/regs/compliance/wh1282.pdf**

Compensation $ense 101

Q How does the Equal Pay Act work?

A The *Equal Pay Act* was passed in 1963 and amended the *FLSA*. It prohibits pay differences between men and women for equal skill, effort and responsibility that are performed under similar working conditions. It has put greater emphasis on job analysis, job documentation, and job evaluation. The *Equal Pay Act* is enforced by the Equal Employment Opportunity Commission, or EEOC. Under the *Equal Pay Act*, four exceptions are allowed for unequal payments:

- Seniority systems
- Merit systems
- A system which measures earnings by quantity or quality of production
- Any factor other than gender

Q How does the Title VII regulation affect compensation?

A *Title VII of the Civil Rights Act* became law in 1964 and has been amended since. It prohibits workplace discrimination on the basis of race, color, religion, gender, or national origin in the hiring, firing, training, compensation, or promotion of employees. *Title VII* covers employers who employ 15 or more employees for 20 or more weeks per year. It is enforced by the EEOC. Employees or applicants can file a discrimination complaint; and the EEOC can come in on the assumption there is a problem to investigate. The burden of proof falls on the employer that no discrimination is occurring.

Q Who is covered by the Age Discrimination Act?

A Passed in 1967, this *Act* protects workers aged 40 and over from employment discrimination with respect to compensation terms, conditions, or privileges of employment. Additionally, it prohibits the following:

- Mandatory retirement with some exceptions
- Limiting or classifying employees in any way related to their age
- Reducing any employee's wage to comply with the *Act*
- Indicating any preference based on age in notices of employment

The *Age Discrimination Act* is enforced by the EEOC

Q **What does the *Consumer Credit Protection Act* cover?**

A Also called the *Wage Garnishment Act*, the *Consumer Credit Protection Act* was passed in 1968. It regulates wage *garnishments* and covers all employees. The *Act* draws a distinction between garnishments for support obligations and garnishments for other debts, with separate maximums allowed in each case. Garnishments are typically received and administered by the payroll department of an employer and are considered confidential.

Q **How does the *Americans with Disabilities Act* affect compensation?**

A The *Americans with Disabilities Act* was passed in 1992. It requires employers to extend equal opportunities to individuals with disabilities in all aspects of employment including hiring, advancement, compensation and training. Employers are further required to provide reasonable accommodation for persons with disabilities who are otherwise qualified for the job unless making the accommodation poses an undue hardship for the employer or the individual poses a direct threat to the health or safety of others in the workplace. Persons who can perform the essential functions of a job with or without *reasonable accommodation* are considered qualified and protected from employment discrimination under the law. Thus, it is very important your job descriptions clearly define the essential functions of each job.

Q **What is the *Lilly Ledbetter Fair Pay Act*?**

A This *Act* was passed in 2009. It affects employers with 15 or more employees. Under this *Act*, each paycheck can trigger a new potential discriminatory act; and an unlawful practice occurs when a person is affected by a discriminatory pay decision or other practice. This law was retroactive to May 28, 2007, and applied to all pay discrimination claims that were pending on or after that date.

continued

As an employer, you must document and be able to defend new hire, merit, promotion, and all other compensation decisions. As a rule-of-thumb, you should retain compensation-related documents for 10 to 20 years. Train your supervisors and managers concerning performance evaluation decisions and salary adjustments. Simply put, consistency and fairness are key. Encourage employees to come to the Human Resources department with pay issues by encouraging honest and trusting relationships through various employee communication strategies. Conducting an Internal Equity Analysis on a regular basis is important to identify any potential discrimination.

See additional information in the chapter on *Base Pay*.

Q What is a Compensation Audit, and why should we conduct one?

A A Compensation Audit is an *internal* review that helps your organization ensure it is in compliance with all federal and state laws covering compensation and pay practices. (A *Compliance* Audit, on the other hand, is an external compliance review conducted by a regulatory agency.)

Areas typically reviewed in a Compensation Audit include the following:

- Compensation philosophy
- Job descriptions
- *FLSA* exemption status (which determines overtime eligibility) for all jobs
- Base pay structure
- How jobs are benchmarked
- How the work week is defined
- How various employee categories are defined
- How work time is documented
- Other areas to help ensure compliance with wage and hour laws as well as posting requirements

Q Can we expect a Department of Labor audit?

A Navigating employee compensation can be complex and overwhelming. And with increasing numbers of Department of Labor (DOL) audits and *FLSA* suits, well, it can get downright scary. Of course, it can be a lot less frightening if you are confident your company's Employee Compensation Plan can stand up to regulatory scrutiny. Perhaps a DOL audit is not in your near-term future, but can you be sure? Can you be certain that a claim filed by an employee – current or former – would not trigger an investigation? Are you confident that your employee compensation plan is up-to-date and in compliance with ever-changing regulatory mandates? Let's look at some factors that could place your company at risk, and what you can do about them:

Escalating Risks

The number of *FLSA* cases filed against employers has risen steadily, and these claims must be investigated by the Department of Labor. Even if your Compensation Plan is fundamentally sound, your company could be found liable for violations if the implementation and administration of the plan is inconsistent.

What are some of the reasons for the escalating numbers of *FLSA* lawsuits? They appear to fall into 6 key areas:

- Outdated federal statutes written decades ago
- Poorly-defined and ambiguous terms in regulations that impact compensation plan understanding and administration
- State laws
- Large lawsuit settlement payouts that encourage more litigation
- A general increase in public awareness about employee rights and regulations
- Talk of raising the minimum wage making employees more conscious of wage and hour laws and their rights under these laws

continued

FLSA Classification Pitfalls

One big risk factor increasing the likelihood of an *FLSA* suit and DOL audit can be found in your *employee classifications*. For example, classifying management trainees or interns as exempt or forgetting to include non-discretionary bonuses in overtime pay. Whether or not an employee is engaged with your computer systems also comes into play, as does the Bachelor's degree "auto qualifier."

Common staff misclassifications include:

- Secretaries and Administrative Assistants
- Help desk personnel
- Inside salespersons
- Mortgage Originators
- First-level supervisors
- Event coordinators
- Any positions you don't want to pay overtime

Q How can we reduce the risk of a Department of Labor audit?

A First, do an employee classification audit yourself. Conduct a position-by-position review to make sure your classifications and policies regarding each position and its compensation are in compliance with applicable standards and regulations. Document each job's *qualifying exemption classification*; and write a brief description that clarifies and justifies why the position qualifies under the designated classification. Be sure to do this at least every 2 years.

Next, do a Discrimination Analysis. We will discuss this more in another question. Perform an Equity Analysis, too. We will also discuss this more in another question. Then, make sure your Compensation Plan is well documented. To determine this, answer and address these questions:

- Does your Compensation Plan clearly and simply communicate employee incentives?
- Do you include position eligibility?
- Do you include an *"at-will" employment* statement?
- Does your Plan documentation include what objectives are included in the plan and how the objectives are measured?
- Does your Plan documentation include how you determine the incentive payout amount and how often (and when) payouts occur?
- Does your Plan documentation include terms and conditions regarding transfers and terminations, disability and death, payment reviews or reversals?
- Does it spell out how and when Plan modifications are made?

Finally, make sure you keep your documentation – including the above items as well as any from past audits – easily findable and retrievable. Train your managers to take all compensation inquiries seriously, and to commit to timely communication and resolution. Keep all documentation for 15 years or even longer (a 7-year retention plan is no longer sufficient).

We've received an investigatory letter from the Department of Labor informing us they will be auditing our Compensation Plan. How can we prepare for this?

The DOL audit is something every Human Resource professional dreads; and being caught unprepared can create a great amount of work and distress for you and your team. What's more, the actual audit can negatively affect normal business operations because the process is both stressful and time-consuming. Worse yet, being selected for a DOL audit can have serious consequences, as nearly 3 out of 4 investigations result in penalties or require other corrective action.

continued

Many new cases are opened due to employee complaints, primarily concerning job descriptions and non-exempt employee pay. Keep in mind the U.S. Department of Labor can audit how employers pay employees at any time. The DOL has previously targeted employers in low-wage industries for wage and hour violations, particularly in the areas of agriculture, day care establishments, restaurants, garment manufacturing, guard services, health care, hotels and motels, janitorial services, and temporary help.

There are several things employers can do to be ready for a DOL audit. As with any situation, however, prevention is better than remedy. In other words, the best time for an employer to analyze whether it is ready for a DOL audit is *before* the DOL comes knocking.

To be proactive, consider conducting an internal company "self-audit" that includes the following:

- Reviewing job descriptions
- Understanding the differences between federal and state laws and ensuring the laws are correctly applied to employees
- Ensuring *FLSA* classifications are correct
- Keeping accurate payroll records
- Applying policies consistently
- Making sure all records are complete and working to resolve any inconsistencies
- Determining how to address any areas of concern identified via the self-audit
- Examining the pay of all protected classes within every job title

If you do find yourself the subject of a DOL Audit, here are some tips for making the audit process as smooth as possible:

1. Gather Data

The DOL will be specific about what they are auditing and what they want to see. They provide little advance notice of an audit but you can request time to gather records. Typically, the amount of time granted will depend on the auditor. With a wage and hour audit, an investigation typically consists of the following steps:

- Examination of records to determine which laws or exemptions apply. These records include, for example, those showing the employer's annual dollar volume of business transactions, involvement in interstate commerce, and work on government contracts.
- Examination of payroll and time records; and taking notes or making transcriptions or photocopies essential to the investigation.
- Interviews with certain employees in private. The purpose of these interviews is to verify the employer's payroll and time records, to identify workers' particular duties in sufficient detail to decide which exemptions apply, if any, and to confirm that minors are legally employed.

2. Review Data

Before handing over a single record to the DOL, review it first to determine if any adjustments are in order and identify this. Keep in mind that non-compliance means the possibility of back pay being owed to former or current employees, as well as the potential for fines and penalties. To lessen the potential impact, compare job descriptions to actual work performed and pay data. If you find errors, fix them immediately.

continued

3. *Ensure onsite time is smooth*

You can help limit the time an investigator is onsite by having your data prepared and in an easy-to-review format, having your employees who will be interviewed present and ready, and answering any questions in a timely manner. If possible, designate one or two company representatives to work with the auditor. This can be the company's legal counsel, or even senior managers. The representatives will have the duty to provide documents requested, arrange for any additional records to be provided to the auditor, and coordinate employee interviews. And don't forget to be courteous and cooperate with the auditor.

4. *Fix any violations*

A DOL audit isn't closed until violations have been corrected. When all fact-finding steps have been completed, the investigator will tell you whether violations have occurred and, if so, what they are and how to correct them. For example, if the audit proves you have been paying overtime incorrectly, you must fix that immediately and pay any back wages as the DOL determines. Then you must keep your pay practices in line with regulations going forward.

Remember this: the most important things you can do to avoid an audit altogether is listen to your employees, ensure they are being paid properly and fairly, and correct any errors as they arise.

What is an OFCCP audit?

The OFCCP is the Office of Federal Contract Compliance. They ensure employers doing business with the federal government are in compliance with non-discrimination and affirmative action laws and regulations. If your company deals with federal contracts, you will be under the scrutiny of the OFCCP. Most frequent findings and financial settlements are against companies for hiring discrimination, compensation, and reasonable accommodation. Ensure your selection process does not adversely affect or unfairly favor a class of protected individuals. Also watch out for discrimination against "non-protected" classes. For example, if it appears whites or males are statistically disfavored, investigate the same as you would if it were women or minorities.

Q **What is an Internal Equity Analysis?**

A An *Internal Equity Analysis* makes sure employees in the same classification, job title and/or pay grade are being paid equitably. Make certain any wide variations in compensation can be supported by mitigating factors such as education, previous related experience, time in job, and performance. Perform this analysis at least annually to identify any potential discrimination issues that you could correct prior to a DOL or OFCCP audit.

Q **What is a Discrimination Analysis?**

A This analysis is a review, by job, of all protected classes (age, gender, race, and disability) to uncover large differences in compensation. This analysis can be done as a stand-alone analysis or in conjunction with an Internal Equity Analysis. You should perform a *Discrimination Analysis* annually to uncover any potential discrimination issues you could correct.

Q **What does compensation have to do with the FMLA?**

A Whether you or a family member has taken advantage of it or not, you are probably familiar with the *Family and Medical Leave Act*, or *FMLA*. Here's how the *FMLA* impacts your compensation program in two key areas:

The first compensation decision you will make regarding *FMLA* is whether an employee is eligible to receive pay when on an approved *FMLA* leave. This is important whether the employee has exhausted their short-term disability pay or is on a leave for other than their own medical reason (and will thus, not receive short-term disability benefits). If your organization decides to allow employees to receive pay while on a *FMLA* leave, the next question is: "Where will the pay come from?" Will it come from the employee's "sick pay" allotment? From their vacation pay? Will you require an employee to use a certain amount – or even all – of their sick time before they can use vacation time? Or will you allow an employee to retain their sick time and immediately debit their vacation time?

continued

A similar situation also arises when an employee is on an approved *FMLA* leave for the birth of a child and they exhaust their short-term disability benefits but are still able to take more *FMLA* time up to the maximum 12 weeks. Once an employee has received their maximum disability benefits, will you then allow them to use other paid time for the remaining 12 weeks they can be on leave? Obviously, many different scenarios and possible policy solutions can come into play.

The second compensation decision you will make is how employees who receive commissions, bonuses, or incentives will be paid while on *FMLA* leave. The law requires that employees maintain their eligibility for these compensation programs while on *FMLA* leave, but how you pay under each type of compensation program may vary. For example, employees on commission programs should be paid according to how your commission plan defines *when* they earn a commission. If they earn a commission and are subsequently on an *FMLA* leave before they are paid the commission, you would certainly want to pay the commission while they are away on an approved *FMLA* leave. If an employee is in a bonus or incentive program, however, you might want different language in those plans about compensation while on an *FMLA* leave. The language might differ, too, based on compensation plan parameters and whether the measure is an individual or team metric.

Ultimately, because each compensation plan and each of its parameters are unique to your company, it is important for your organization to have a policy addressing how employees can be paid while on an approved *FMLA* leave, and that you consistently follow it for all *FMLA* leaves.

ROI of Compensation

In this section you will learn about...

Employees as an Investment

Competitive Compensation

Employee Turnover Cost

Total Rewards Strategic Assessment

Compensation Scorecard

Employer vs Employee Markets

Attracting and Retaining Talent

Compensation Review

Total Compensation Review

Sales Compensation Scorecard

NOTE: Terms in *red italics* in the following text are defined in the Glossary.

Q **What is *"ROI of compensation"*?**

A The Return on Investment (ROI) of Compensation can be measured in many ways which are explored in this chapter. Turnover, replacement costs, and engaged employees are also important measurements of your return on investment in compensation. Additionally, how your numbers compare to your compensation philosophy is an important return on investment measure.

Q **Why is it important to measure the ROI of compensation?**

A It is important to measure and track the ROI of all your compensation programs to help determine if they are working and cost effective as designed, implemented and managed. When measuring the ROI of your compensation programs, include money spent externally or internally to develop or enhance those programs. Indeed, most development or analysis costs typically pay for themselves in cost avoided for just one turnover, or in more efficient ways of acquiring new employees or dealing with disengaged employees. Several ways to measure your compensation programs are included in this chapter.

Why is it important to view employees as an investment rather than an expense?

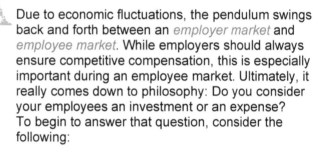 Due to economic fluctuations, the pendulum swings back and forth between an *employer market* and *employee market*. While employers should always ensure competitive compensation, this is especially important during an employee market. Ultimately, it really comes down to philosophy: Do you consider your employees an investment or an expense? To begin to answer that question, consider the following:

- Are you going to be able to attract and retain top talent?
- Do you say your employees are your most valuable asset? If so, is this true?
- How are employees getting ahead in your organization?
- How does your total rewards program (compensation, benefits, work/life) measure up to your competition?
- Are you retaining customers?
- What is your return on investment (ROI) as it relates to investments in employees?
- Do your employees trust your organization?

It is essential to ensure many of your Human Resources (HR) practices are designed and aligned to attract and retain top talent. *To achieve that goal, employers must see their employees as an investment and not an expense.* Of course, viewing employees as investments means you will need to make investments IN your employees. These can take many forms, from compensation to benefits to technology improvements to training or career development.

To enhance your chances of landing top talent in a competitive hiring marketplace, your compensation package will need to be on par with, or better than, your competitors. To make sure that is true, check the value of jobs in your market. This will provide data necessary to indicate if your company's compensation programs are on target or need adjustment.

Moving to an employee market might mean your compensation programs need upgrading. If you want to be a marketplace leader, one that can attract and retain superior talent, you'll need to position your company at or near the top of your industry's compensation and rewards programs. If your business model is one that can withstand more frequent employee turnover, you can adjust your compensation programs accordingly. But remember this: the cost of employee turnover is typically from 1.5 to 3 times the employee's annual salary. Constant employee churn will be costly!

Consider your other programs (besides merit) that can help your top performers get ahead. Can you differentiate your total reward programs (both compensation and benefits) from your competitors? And can you help employees quantify these differences in total compensation?

Simply put, beyond employee pay, remaining competitive in an employee-favorable economy might require well-crafted incentive and reward programs. These can include referral bonuses for employees who recommend desirable recruits, signing bonuses when top talent comes on board, and performance incentives to inspire productivity and results. You can also consider loyalty bonuses for top performers you don't want to lose. The right components of an effective rewards program should be unique to your company and industry.

Measurement systems are also important. These can help you identify if your employee investments are paying off. Key measurement questions can include the following:

- What are your sales or profitability per employee this year compared to last?
- Have your investments in employees paid for themselves in productivity improvements?
- Are you retaining customers?
- How do you know if your employees trust your company and their manager? (Many employees "quit" their manager before they will quit the company.)
- Are your managers spending time with top performers and working to meet their needs?

continued

89

Deciding whether to view your employees as an investment or an expense is fundamental to how you shape your compensation philosophy, policies, practices and processes. I firmly believe that companies who consider their employees an investment have a sustainable competitive advantage in any marketplace.

Q How can competitive employee compensation benefit my company?

A Competitive employee compensation isn't just an admirable goal or lofty ideal; if you want your company to attract and retain top talent and improve employee morale, competitive compensation is a must.

To determine if your employee compensation program is competitive, answer these questions:

- Do you have trouble recruiting top-notch performers in your industry?
- Have you lost excellent employees to key competitors due to pay or other compensation components?
- Does your company suffer from poor productivity and low morale based on perceptions – right or wrong – that pay is too low?
- Are your incentive programs not driving desired employee productivity and behaviors?
- Do your top performers feel undervalued?
- Are company loyalty and commitment suffering among longer-term employees because they believe new hires are being paid more than they are despite their years of service?
- Do you lack confidence that your "*merit dollars*" are being utilized effectively?
- Do you feel your company has skills gaps that cannot be filled within your current compensation structure?

If you answered "yes" to even a few of these questions, your employee compensation may be a major part of the problem. On the other hand, if your company maintains competitive employee compensation as part of a well-crafted compensation program – and your employees know this to be true – there are many benefits to be realized. These can include better overall productivity and individual employee performance, greater employee satisfaction and morale, and improved employee loyalty.

With market-correct employee compensation programs in place, you can more confidently and cost-effectively recruit top industry talent. You can reduce costs due to employee turnover. And you can improve job descriptions and identify skills gaps, training needs, and development opportunities. You'll even be able to more accurately determine which employees are eligible for overtime pay (and perhaps even avoid costly *Fair Labor Standards Act [FLSA]* infractions).

How can I use an effective compensation program to attract and retain talent?

Employee attraction and retention are always top-of-mind considerations for most organizations because building a talented, dedicated team is vital to organizational success. Of course, a large part of this responsibility falls on the HR department. Often, HR professionals have in their arsenal attractive benefits packages that include health insurance and retirement plan options. But with an ever-changing economy and insurance landscape, what does an attraction and retention future look like if benefits are no longer a part of compensation?

Consider these best practices used by successful businesses:

1. Base salary on the market.

A common business mistake is to determine salary based on the company's budget rather than on market realities. If a potential employee in a starting position in your industry normally makes $15 an hour, why would someone want to accept the same position in your company for just $10 an hour?

continued

2. Make lifestyle part of your employee recruitment offer.

Many employees are just as concerned about quality of life as they are about the amount of money a position offers. If you offer flexible hours, work-from-home options or other scheduling perks that make work/life balance easier, make sure potential employees know this. And play up attractive features about your city, such as amenities, schools, entertainment options, etc. These lifestyle perks can help attract top employees.

3. Be creative with perks.

As typical perks become less feasible for even large corporations to offer, get creative with other options that can improve the health and wellness of your employees. Offer an on-site health facility, create a walking path around your campus, or offer memberships to your local gym or spa.

4. Show employees they have a future with the company.

Most employees don't envision joining a company and doing the same thing for the next few decades. So, be sure to showcase opportunities for education and advancement in your recruitment efforts. What will the position offer? Will it provide the new employee the chance to learn new skills, or can it be a stepping stone to a position with more responsibilities? Spell this out during the interview process so potential employees can see a long-term future with you.

5. Create an employee incentive program.

An *employee incentive program* not only rewards performance; it also gives prospective employees something to look forward to. Whether it's an annual company-paid retreat or a program where employees collect points they can trade in for cash or paid time off, an employee incentive program can motivate existing employees and help you attract the talent you want on your team.

6. Let money talk.

Consider options for compensation that aren't part of the annual salary. Sometimes a sign-on bonus is all it takes when competition for employees is fierce (with a stipulation of being awarded after a certain length of employment to protect your company from those who might start just for the bonus and then leave). Profit sharing is another option. It's not for every business, but there's no better way to give employees a stake in the company's success. For businesses that look like they're going somewhere, profit sharing programs can be a powerful inducement to come work for you instead of for someone else. You can also consider asking employees for cost savings ideas – and rewarding them for those ideas by sharing in the annual savings generated.

Our employee turnover cost is high. What can we do about it?

If you think you understand the high cost of employee turnover, think again. Many experts believe the cost of replacing skilled and specialized employees to be well above the employee's annual salary. Even the cost associated with replacing entry-level employees can cut deeply into your compensation and employee rewards budget. Let's look at why employees might "jump ship" in the first place, how big an impact that can have on your organization, and what you can do to minimize the impact.

In many cases, company management cannot control why employees choose to leave. Family and personal situations, spousal relocations, opportunities in a new field of interest, and many other reasons can prompt an employee to move on. (They might hit the lottery and buy a remote private island!) But management might be able to mitigate the situation when employees leave for other reasons. These include situations where the employee does not feel engaged with the company's big-picture work. Or if the employee doesn't feel valued for his or her work contributions. Or if the employee can't see a professional development career path within the organization. Or, certainly, if employees incorrectly perceive their salaries to be below market. Many of these situations can be addressed internally with better communication and transparency.

continued

Regardless of why an employee leaves, understand that the cost to your company can be huge – crippling, even. In fact, the cost to replace an employee could range from 20 percent to 400 percent of an employee's annual salary, depending, of course, on many factors, including employee skill level and market availability of replacement workers. Even if your employee turnover costs are lower – helped by finely tuned recruiting and hiring processes, along with rapid and proven onboarding – your company takes a hit every time you replace an employee.

Consider this example of employee turnover cost.

You have 50 terminations in a given year: 70% (or 35) of those are entry-level employees and 30% (or 15) are mid-level employees.

35 entry-level terminations at an average annual salary of $30,000 at 20% turnover cost would cost you $210,000.

15 mid-level terminations at an average annual salary of $65,000 at 150% turnover cost (and this is a conservative number) would cost you $1,462,500.

Combined, your turnover cost for 50 terminations is $1,672,500 – almost $1.7M dollars! Imagine what you could do with that money if it were available for compensation and benefits.

Obviously, if you reduce your *employee churn rate* overall, you reduce the costs associated with replacement. So how can you be better positioned to hold on to valuable workers?

- First, let them know they are valued. This can be as simple as telling employees you appreciate their efforts, individually and as a team.
- Keep them engaged and connected to the big-picture importance of what they are doing for the organization.
- If possible within your organization structure, pro-vide paths for advancement. Don't make promis-es you can't keep, of course, but let employees know there is room to grow inside the organiza-tion and that their loyalty could prove worthwhile.

- Provide personal and professional development opportunities. While this could help prepare a worker for an opportunity outside your organization, it will at least keep them on your team during the development cycle. This will likely yield performance benefits for your company and position the employee's internal advancement opportunities.

- Make sure they are being paid equitably relative to the market, and that they are positioned correctly within their pay grade. If they are too low relative to other workers or due to their own length of service or skill set, you might be able to bump them to a higher percentile.

- When awarding merit increases or year-end bonuses, deliver these rewards in terms of dollars, not percentages. A stated $500 bonus is typically more appreciated than a 1% bonus, even if they are the same reward.

Employees are savvy at seeking information about where they stand in the marketplace and finding opportunities *outside* your organization. Are you as knowledgeable in that regard? Do you have enough market rate information to appreciate the likelihood that employees might leave? If not, it might be time for a *Market Rate Analysis* (typically a good idea at least every two years). Are you confident that your pay grades are appropriately aligned? If not, perhaps a *Pay System Review* is necessary. And are you confident your employees are positioned appropriately within their pay grades? If not, it might be time for an *Internal Equity Analysis*.

Organizations are dynamic things. Employees come and go. Some will find opportunities inside your company while others seek opportunities elsewhere. But because some employee defections are avoidable – and the cost of replacing an employee can be so astronomical – it can be easy to justify compensation analyses and programs that put you in a better position to avoid the high cost of employee turnover.

Why would my company need an employee Compensation Review?

Although the word "review" can strike fear in the hearts of many, a Compensation Review can be a very good – and necessary – thing to keep your company competitive in the marketplace and safely in regulatory compliance. Here's why it is essential to have a periodic Compensation Review:

First and foremost, a comprehensive and professional Compensation Review can help ensure your organization is not at risk of running afoul of important federal and state regulations. For example, your review can substantiate your compliance (or spotlight areas of non-compliance) with:

- *Fair Labor Standards Act (FLSA)* regulations (in conjunction with a Market Analysis)
- Overtime pay practices
- Appropriate tax forms, such as the W-4, W-9, etc.
- Minimum wage laws
- Generally accepted good recordkeeping practices
- Employee notification and posting requirements
- Well-defined and documented employee compensation policies

With a Compensation Review, you typically will receive a summary of findings that can help you understand what actions your company needs to take concerning your compensation practices and policies. If you choose to do a Market Analysis as well, this can help you understand where your company is positioned compared to industry competitors. This can be especially important if you have a higher than desirable turnover rate and/or difficulty attracting and hiring top talent in your industry.

Q **What are the primary areas of focus for a Compensation Review?**

A A Compensation Review should include a look at philosophy, structure, market pricing, merit increases, policies, any compensation analysis completed, litigation, and compliance. The goal, of course, is to position your company to avoid risks and help you achieve or maintain a confident position in your market.

Many companies stay on course regarding employee compensation without truly knowing if the course was the right one in the first place. What's more, many organizations only address critical areas of compliance when a regulatory agency comes calling. These practices can be costly – and can threaten the survival of the business.

It doesn't have to be that way, of course.

A Compensation Review can give you confidence you are positioned to make the right moves for employee compensation and total rewards. Whether you emerge from the review with flying colors or learn you have areas for improvement, you will enjoy peace of mind knowing where you stand. From there, you can take the necessary steps to maintain or enhance your compliance and market competitiveness.

Q **What is a Total Rewards Strategic Assessment, and why does a company need one?**

A Before undertaking a *Total Rewards Strategic Assessment*, it helps to understand its goals and objectives. Those typically are:

- Understanding the total rewards philosophy and practices currently being used as part of the overall total rewards program; and determining the level of consistency between practices, policies and actions compared to the philosophy and vision for the culture.

- Reviewing and assessing current methodologies that support the total rewards philosophy, practices, policies, and procedures to determine alignment with those aspects. This might include methodologies such as survey sources, relevant markets, etc.

continued

- Gathering information regarding desired future direction for total rewards for the next few years. This can help determine gaps between your current philosophy and your desired future philosophy, so recommendations can be made for how to reach that desired state.
- Creating a roadmap and recommendations that outline the steps and details necessary to update and revise the total rewards program.

Key components typically reviewed are designed to provide actionable data and insights. Key areas reviewed as part of a Total Rewards Strategic Assessment include:

- A comprehensive organization assessment, including management interviews
- Compensation, including a review of practices around base pay, variable pay, and reward/recognition programs
- Benefits, including a Competitive Market Assessment
- Performance management and employee development programs
- Communications and training media and methods used to educate staff and stakeholders on all areas included in this review

A Total Rewards Strategic Assessment provides an objective analysis that benchmarks your critical HR functions, and enables you to move forward confidently with your compensation and benefit programs as you operate in a challenging marketplace.

What is a Total Compensation Review?

A *Total Compensation Review* consists of an evaluation of both compensation and benefits to the organization. The compensation piece is accomplished by market benchmarking every role in your organization for both base pay and incentive compensation. You will want to group your jobs by various employee levels (e.g. non-exempt, exempt professional/technical, supervisor, manager, etc.).

You will then develop a report to show the overall comparison by employee group as to where they sit as a percent of market. This analysis can be completed by department or division and then rolled up to the entire company level.

The compensation analysis will help you see how each group of employees compares to market by department/division and company-wide, so you can determine how it aligns (or doesn't align) with your compensation philosophy. The analysis can also help you plan where you need to budget and spend to better align with your compensation philosophy. Thus, it provides leaders a clear picture of where their areas stand, as well as the company as a whole.

The evaluation of benefits to market is a little more complex in order to determine a true mathematical percent-to-market comparison. You should utilize a national human capital consulting firm with a database of employee benefit plan details for your industry. It is possible you could get a comparison to your competitors if there is a sufficient quantity of them in the database. This analysis will compare your benefit plan offerings and design details to market for each major benefit area and then provide you an overall percent to market for your benefits. As an example, you might come out of the analysis at 85% to market or 105% of market. The combination of these two analyses – a Market Rate Analysis and a Benefit Design Analysis – provides a robust Total Compensation Review for your organization.

Q How can we evaluate our compensation programs?

A It is important to frequently determine if your compensation programs are effective, efficient and appropriate for your organization. After all, things change! That's why it is important to ask and answer these questions:

continued

- Is your compensation program meeting the objectives established by management?
- How do you know? What are your metrics? (We will discuss more on metrics in some upcoming questions.)
- Is the compensation program being administered according to employer policies and procedures?
- Can the plans withstand the risk of challenge from employees, government agencies, and other third parties?
- Is there an understanding of the roles and responsibilities between HR and line managers in the administration of compensation plans?
- Is there continuous evaluation for future program enhancements or modifications by determining both what is important to the employee versus how satisfied they are?

Knowing the gaps between importance and satisfaction on various compensation programs, benefit programs, or any other HR programs can help ensure you address the biggest gaps.

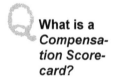 **What is a Compensation Scorecard?**

 A well-crafted and comprehensive Compensation Scorecard not only describes your company's various compensation program components; it also is a great tool to help management measure and benchmark progress and performance year over year. To stay on course and market-competitive with your compensation and total rewards programs, you must measure, measure, measure! This means you must track and measure against your compensation philosophy, as well as effective business drivers and results. Here's why a Compensation Scorecard can be so valuable:

First, understand that your company's Compensation Scorecard can be created at – and directed toward – various levels in the organization. These include the organization level, division level, department level, or even an employee group level (such as non-exempt, exempt professional, exempt technical, etc.).

The scorecard can include several different types of measurements. For example, one measurement can be *percent-to-market* if you have a market-based compensation system, or *percent-to-midpoint* if you have a pay range compensation system. You can report metrics for your entire organization and then break them down into the levels mentioned above. Keep in mind that these metrics can be more meaningful and valuable to management when tightly focused toward each group.

Approached this way, the measurements can help you see how each group is being paid relative to your company-wide compensation philosophy. For example, if your aim is to pay on average at 100% of prevailing market compensation rates, but you have a group being compensated at 85% of market, that group is said to be "under market". If another group is paid at 120% of prevailing market rates, then your compensation program for that group is "over market". Thus, these metrics can help you see which groups, if any, are out of line with the market and/or your company norm.

Another good measurement is *average incentive pay per department*. This metric can help you see which groups are getting the largest – and the smallest – average incentive pay. Knowing this can help senior management compare how well the organization's divisions or departments are performing. What's more, if an area is known to be high-performing but is not getting a high level of incentive compensation as compared to other groups, this could indicate that something is wrong with your incentive compensation program.

continued

Average merit rating per department is another valuable metric. This measurement, in the context of the company's overall average ratings, can help management recognize the correlation between performance measurement and merit awards. It can also indicate if some managers are more generous in their ratings than others.

Turnover and retention analyses are also good tools and can help you evaluate compensation as well. High turnover in a particular area might indicate a possible compensation issue. If you ask about compensation in exit interviews this information is also helpful. Additionally, a review of *costs versus budget* as well as *results versus objectives* can also be good indicators of how well your compensation plans are performing.

These and other benchmarks can paint a clear picture for management to help monitor various phases of your company's compensation system. Simply put, if you have compensation plans in your organization, you need a Compensation Scorecard. With a well-designed Compensation Scorecard in place, your business and your employees can come out winners.

Q What are effective measures for a *Sales Compensation Scorecard?*

A Differentiation can help you determine if your top sales compensation earners are also truly your top sales performers. Be sure to build into your measurement criteria the necessary performance differentiation data to make this assessment.

Among measures to consider when using a Sales Compensation Scorecard to evaluate the effectiveness of your sales compensation program are:

- *Total Cash Compensation Comp-a-ratio*: Determining how your salesperson total compensation compares to market or your desired total cash compensation at target can let your organization know how competitive your Sales Compensation Plan is.

- *Compensation Cost of Sales:* The total compensation dollars paid as a percent of sales.
- *Pay and Performance Correlation:* Use a scattergram to illustrate each sales representative's incentive pay versus revenue generated; this can help you discover any misalignment between top performers and top earners.
- *Distribution of Representative Earnings:* Use a bar chart measure to validate if the plan is functioning as expected showing percentages of the sales representative's hitting below target, at target and above target.
- *Percent of Sales/Percent of Quota Earnings:* This measure can help you uncover any disconnects between the quarterly percent of sales plan earned and the average percent of quota earned. For example, if sales for Q2 are at 105% and the average quota earned is at 70%, something is amiss. The same would be true for the reverse situation. In either case, such results should raise questions for the business unit about possible extraordinary factors such as short-term revenue windfalls, shortfalls, design issues, etc.

What if I do not have the necessary expertise in sales compensation to analyze and evaluate it?

Proper compensation for the salesperson requires more than just careful analysis and structure. It also requires proper communication and constant monitoring and adjustments. Obviously, salesperson compensation can be complex, with many moving parts. The larger your organization or industry, or the more diverse your product or service offerings, the more complicated it becomes to design, monitor and fine tune your sales compensation program. If you have no experience in this area, seek help from an outside compensation consultant with expertise in designing sales compensation plans as well as analyzing and evaluating plans.

Communicating About Compensation

In this section you will learn about...

Employee Beliefs About Pay

Sharing Pay Information

Best Communication Practices

Advice for Managers

Effects of Misperceptions

Communicating Cost Reductions

Handling Bad Compensation News

NOTE: Terms in *red italics* in the following text are defined in the Glossary.

What is "compensation communication"?

Compensation communication is simply the process of keeping employees and others affected by employee compensation and total rewards informed. When communicating about compensation it is important to use appropriate communication channels to ensure they get the information. Of course, it is also critical to make compensation messaging crystal clear.

Why is communicating about compensation important?

Many employees feel compensation is a "black box" or a secret. The less employees know about your compensation processes, the more skeptical they are about compensation being competitive. I am not suggesting you post everyone's pay rate, but the more transparent you can be about your compensation processes, the more the black box perception disappears. The bottom line is about trust. If employees know the processes and methodologies used to establish and manage compensation – and they understand them – they will trust the process and management.

A well-designed and understood compensation communication approach also ensures employees have accurate expectations regarding their pay. This, in turn, has a positive impact on motivation, retention, and performance.

Q **Why do most employees believe they are paid below market rate?**

A It's about perception – and don't forget that perception IS reality. Both affect employee work and loyalty.

The reality is that most workers believe they are being paid below market rate regardless of where they actually stand compared to their peers. Another significant reality is that this perception negatively impacts not only how engaged these workers are in the workplace, but also their intentions of staying with their current employer. That's the bad news. The good news is this: you can take steps to change employee perceptions and, in the process, help create a workplace culture of satisfaction and loyalty.

Consider this: In the fall of 2015, PayScale surveyed 71,000 workers about this subject and the findings were reported in a *Harvard Business Review* article. The survey broke its results into three groups of respondents: those who were being paid above market, at market, and below market. For those being paid at or above market rate, the clear majority believed they were being paid less relative to market than they actually were being paid. Case in point: some 80% of workers who were really being paid above market believed they were either being paid below market (35%) or at market (45%). In other words, only about 1 in 5 employees at this level truly understood they were being paid above market. Likewise, of those respondents who were truly being paid at market rate, nearly two-thirds (64%) believed they were being paid below market. The only respondents who seemed to accurately understand their compensation relative to their actual market rate position were those workers being paid below market; 83% perceived (correctly) that they were being paid below market.

Q **What effect does employee perception of compensation really have?**

A According to the *Harvard Business Review* article, worker perception affects their engagement, satisfaction, and ultimately, loyalty. Not surprisingly, pay is a huge factor in employee motivation, engagement and performance. The perception that pay is too low makes the employee feel undervalued and underappreciated. This, of course, leads to job dissatisfaction and to seeking opportunities elsewhere. And of course, when an employee leaves an organization, the company incurs significant costs to hire, train and assimilate a new employee.

Communicating About Compensation

Q: What can be done to curb employee misperceptions about pay?

A: By openly and honestly sharing market rate information with employees, your company can align perception with reality. You can assure employees they are probably better off compared to the marketplace than they thought. And even if you are paying below market, you can explain why that pay position is necessary (e.g., corporate financial setbacks, other elements of compensation that offset lower pay, etc.). Of course, if you have not done a recent *Market Benchmark Analysis*, you won't be in a good position to communicate positively with employees.

Q: What compensation information is typically shared with an employee?

A: It is wise to transparently communicate with employees as much information as your organization is comfortable sharing. Some common information shared with employees may include the following:

- Career paths
- Minimum and mid-point of a pay range
- The employee's own pay range
- Growth opportunity
- Salary ranges for posted jobs
- Incentive program expectations and specific rewards
- Incentive plan documentation details when available

Q: How does an organization determine what is appropriate to communicate?

A: Communication about compensation within organizations can be controversial. Some companies have total transparency regarding compensation while others hold information "close to the vest", revealing little to nothing about compensation. Still others share only bits of information with their employees.

continued

There are two levels of wage transparency to explore. The first level is *Process Transparency*. This is the minimum a company should do if working toward transparency. With the Process Transparency approach, employees understand where companies get their benchmark data, how salaries are determined, what pay scales are for their position, and what it takes to earn more. That is both a good place to start and a good middle ground for employers who may not want to share exact details but want employees to have adequate information regarding compensation plans.

The second level is *Full-salary Transparency*. This approach involves letting employees – and in some cases, the public – know just how much everyone at the company earns. Proponents of open salary policies believe that a culture of shared information helps create a sense of a "shared fate" among employees, as well as reducing discrimination based on gender or other characteristics. And while companies may not like transparency, they cannot keep rank-and-file employees from disclosing their pay internally or externally, under the federal *National Labor Relations Act*. At a time when companies are holding tight to corporate purse strings, employees are becoming increasingly focused on pay fairness.

Ultimately, there are pros and cons to compensation transparency; and companies need to determine what will work best for achieving long-term goals and employee satisfaction.

Q How can I best communicate cost reductions (including layoffs) when the economy is bad?

A In tough economic times, company leaders often target cost reductions. This can include cost savings from layoffs. The important thing to remember is that cost savings from "re-engineering" the workforce (that is, using employee layoffs) cannot be linked to executive bonuses. You will not be able to continue to get employee engagement once the staff finds out that executives were paid bonuses based on cost reductions achieved through layoffs. This is the kind of behavior that causes employees to flee once the economy turns around. Indeed, staff members will recall how they were treated, and more importantly, how executives acted and were paid during tough economic times.

Q **What are some important things to remember when communicating compensation?**

A Use all appropriate communications media to communicate compensation. These might include your company intranet or proprietary portal, mobile messages, printed material, email, meetings, podcasts, and any other medium your workforce uses. Keep in mind how each generation in your workforce prefers specific communication mediums, and target communications to specific demographics when possible. As an example, those close to retirement want to hear a different message about the retirement plan than those who have recently entered the workforce.

Ensure your managers are trained in every aspect of your compensation policies and practices, and that they know *how* to discuss compensation with their employees. Use clear and concise language in all your communications. Before sharing compensation communications with your workforce, ask someone unfamiliar with the content to read through it and provide feedback that will enable you to enhance clarity and conciseness. The same holds true for any plan document created, such as for incentive compensation plans. And finally, obtain senior management buy-in on what your communication philosophy will be around compensation and *how much* you will share with employees.

Q **What is an effective way to communicate your entire compensation philosophy, policies and procedures with managers?**

A An effective way to share the overall plan with your management team is to create a *Manager's Compensation Guide*. Such a *Guide* should include things like the following:

- A compensation overview on principles and philosophy
- The compensation structure (job descriptions, ranges, market pricing to name a few)
- Pay decisions for all types of pay changes and how each type works
- Incentive compensation
- An appendix for any form referenced

Q **What else should be done to effectively communicate your organization's compensation philosophy, policies and procedures to managers?**

A You could conduct a training class for managers that would cover the same material you might put in a *Manager's Compensation Guide*. From a procedural perspective, the training class is not typically as in-depth as the *Guide* might be. The *Guide* provides the same documentation to all managers, and it can be updated when key information changes. A training class, on the other hand, provides the opportunity to more easily answer questions, practice conversations, and address items that may not have been included in the training materials.

If you conduct a training class to communicate compensation, provide all participants a copy of the slides so they have consistent documentation. You may also want to video record the training class and require new managers to watch it as part of their onboarding, as well as making it available to all managers as a refresher. At a minimum, train your managers on the following:

- Your organization's compensation philosophy
- Its guiding principles
- The different elements of compensation
- The compensation benchmarking process and approach
- Guidelines for understanding total compensation for each employee to make good pay decisions
- What the communication processes are for each type of pay decision
- The importance of manager involvement in compensation decisions and discussions with employees

Q **What are some best practices for implementing and commu- nicating sales compensation plans?**

A Effective communication of the salesperson compensation program can help ensure that a newly introduced or modified plan will "hit the ground running." Communication must be timely and clear. This is never more important than when a plan is new, has been modified substantially, or has many component variables. Even the best *Sales Compensation Plan* must be "sold" to the sales employees in the field; as even positive *Plan* changes can fail if communication of those changes is poorly done. Poor communication of the *Plan* also can lead to a reduction of personal productivity, a reduction in overall corporate performance, and even excessive turnover.

Of course, good communication is more than merely delivering a plan document. You'll want to personalize the communication to enhance clarity and buy-in. For best effect, strike the right balance between too much info and too little info. Communicate when people need it, such as when the program is rolled out and before measurements begin. For communicating results, share details and outcomes within a reasonable period after a measurement period closes. (Don't keep your salesperson guessing because this could impact their performance in the new period.)

Q **What is the best way to handle bad news about compensation?**

A Build trust by communicating early (proactively), with clarity, and in the right tone. Clearly convey to affected employees the types, timing, and rationale of changes. Provide sufficient lead time for employees to digest honest and candid information; and be sure to proactively address questions. It is always a best practice to establish ongoing open discussions and communications.

Compensation $ense 101

Q **How should we advise our managers to handle employees who approach them regarding their pay?**

A Managers should, first and foremost, truly listen to the employee and be sure they understand the employee's concerns. Then the manager should ask questions to clarify their concerns; and should ensure they understand all the skills and knowledge the employee possesses relative to the job, as well as how well the employee is performing in their position. The manager should commit to the employee that they will look into their concerns and get back to them. The manager should also let the worker know the company wants to retain good employees and remain competitive in the industry. Any additional "hot skills" needed in this employee's job should be identified by the manager. The manager should then be sure they know the salary range for the employee's job and schedule a meeting with their supervisor to discuss this employee's pay relative to other employees in the same or very similar role.

If a manager and the employee's supervisor feel an increase is warranted, they should work with Human Resources (HR) on a possible pay change. The manager should keep the employee updated on the status of their concern at various points during the continuing investigation. The manager SHOULD NOT make any commitments regarding pay increases or set an expectation they can get back to the employee within 24 hours. However, the manager SHOULD communicate they will move in a timely manner to address the employee's pay concern. In fact, each employee's pay concern must be treated individually. Sometimes, warranted pay increases can require several layers of leadership approval.

Q **How do I know if our compensation communications are working?**

A Regularly revisit your communications to keep them fresh, accurate and relevant. You can also conduct focus group sessions to learn how your compensation communications are perceived in your organization. Finally, determine if your compensation communications align with the organization's value and culture. For example, if a core organizational value is transparency but you are not being transparent when communicating about compensation, your stated values are misaligned with your practices.

Glossary

Common Compensation and Total Rewards Terms

Actual Mix Actual mix represents the pay mix of an employee's compensation typically represented with base pay shown first and then incentive. i.e. 75/25 would indicate 75% of pay is coming from base and 25% is coming from incentives.

Affirmative Action Policy that goes beyond equal employment opportunity by requiring organizations to 1) comply with the law, and 2) correct past discriminatory practices by increasing the numbers of minorities and women in specific classes.

Anniversary-based Method Increase process used where employees receive their merit pay increases on their annual anniversary date.

"At Risk" Pay Pay that is not guaranteed and must be re-earned.

"At Will" Employment Term used in U.S. labor law for contractual employment relationships in which an employee can be dismissed by an employer for any reason, even without establishing "just cause", and without warning.

Baby Boomer Generation Term describing the age group of a person typically born between 1946 and 1964.

Base Pay Financial compensation earned either hourly or on a salary basis. Base pay does not include shift pay, differential pay, holiday pay, overtime pay, or other non-financial benefits or perks.

Benchmarking Process of measuring internal services and practices against recognized industry standards or leaders to identify areas for internal improvement.

Benefits Non-financial compensation that typically includes such things as health insurance, dental insurance, life insurance, retirement plan, and paid time-off that employers provide to employees either at no cost or at a shared cost.

Benefits Philosophy Statement that typically describes an employer's desired position regarding employee benefits compared to market (below, at or above), the amount of employee choice desired to be provided in coverage, any focus on wellness or well-being, and what industry an employer relies on for comparison purposes.

Compensation $ense 101

Bonus Employee compensation derived from a plan with goals typically paid as additional cash as a reward for obtaining plan objectives. *See also "Incentive Pay" and "Incentive Compensation".*

Broadbanding Method of evaluating and constructing a job grading structure. Broad bands typically have very large spreads from minimum to maximum of 100% or more and cover many positions in each band.

Career Development Increase Type of pay increase given for adding either breadth or depth of responsibilities that might not necessarily result in a full pay grade or band change. Often used in conjunction with *Broadbanding*.

Cash Plans Incentive or bonus plan that pays an employee additional cash for achieving objectives.

Commission Methodology for compensating salespeople that may be used as the sole means of compensation or in conjunction with base pay compensation. Typically, a commission is the amount a salesperson earns for selling products or services. It can be a flat dollar amount or a percent of the sale.

Compensation Typically, the direct financial reward or payment made by an employer to an employee in the form of base pay, bonuses, incentives, and/or commissions.

Compensation Life Cycle Correlation of different aspects of compensation (base pay, bonus, etc.) to attraction, engagement, and retention.

Compensation Philosophy Statement that typically describes an employer's desired position regarding compensation compared to market (below, at or above).

Competency-based Pay Pay structure that awards compensation based on the employee's competency levels.

Consumer Price Index Measure of the average change in prices over time of a fixed "market basket" of goods and services.

Cost of Living Amount of money needed to sustain a basic level of living including primary expenses such as food, housing, taxes and healthcare. Often used as a measure for comparing costs associated with living in one city versus another.

Glossary

Cost of Living Adjustment (COLA) Pay adjustment given that is tied to cost of living data.

Cost of Salary Pay that is either more or less when comparing one city to another. Often the same job in a similar type company would pay more or less depending on location due to cost of living and other factors.

Customer Contact Plans Incentive or bonus plans designed for Call Center employees that typically have some team and individual goals.

Discrimination Analysis Analysis completed on protected categories of employees to ensure employee pay is fairly aligned with other protected employee classifications in the same or similar job.

Employee Churn Rate Measure of the speed of employee turnover.

Employee Classifications *Fair Labor Standards Act (FLSA)* classifications used to determine if an employee qualifies for exemption from overtime.

Employee Incentive Program Plan designed to motivate employees to hit goals for which they will receive rewards upon their attainment.

Employee Market Condition existing when there is a scarcity of talent which leads to employees having more leverage negotiating compensation and working conditions.

Employer Market Condition existing when there is an abundance of talent or economic downturn, which leads to the employer having more leverage in negotiating compensation and working conditions.

Equity Increases Pay increase given when an employee is not properly placed in the pay range based on education, skill, performance, etc. or when a large market movement has occurred which warrants an adjustment to employee pay in order to keep the employee on par with market.

Exemption Status Indication of whether a position qualifies for exemption from overtime derived by applying *Fair Labor Standards Act (FLSA)* guidelines.

External Equity Market benchmarking process used to determine the value of employee positions in the market.

Focal Time-based Method Compensation method in which all employees receive their annual pay increases at the same time in the year.

Full Salary Transparency Compensation philosophy and practice in which all employees (and sometimes the public) know how much each employee in an organization earns.

Gain Sharing Incentive Plan Incentive plan based on financial gain only wherein a portion of results over goal are shared with the employee typically in an annual cash payment.

Garnishments Reduction in wages received from an employer for an employee for which the employer must withhold wages. Garnishments are typically for support obligations or other debts.

Generation X Term describing the age group of a person typically born between 1965 and 1980.

Generation Y See *Millennials*.

Generation Z Term describing the age group of a person typically born during the generational period after the mid-1990s. Also known as "The iGeneration".

Goal Sharing Incentive Plan Incentive plan typically implemented organization-wide and focusing on business performance and achieving continuous improvement results. Often a balanced scorecard approach.

Hazard Pay Premium paid to an employee in recognition of working in hazardous conditions such as extreme temperatures or extreme heights.

HRIS Abbreviation for Human Resources Information System; which is a database for gathering and storing employee data and generating reports from the data.

Incentive Compensation Variable rewards designed to stimulate employee performance for achievement of short-term or long-term goals.

Incentive Pay Pay received from an incentive compensation plan. Often referred to as *"variable pay"* as it must be re-earned every measurement period.

Glossary

Internal Equity Utilization of job analysis, job documentation, and job evaluation to determine which jobs are the same or similar.

Internal Equity Analysis/Review Analysis conducted to ensure employee pay is fairly aligned with other employees in the same or similar jobs.

Job Analysis Systematic and formal study of job content which includes the process of obtaining important and relevant information about a job such as knowledge, experience, tasks, equipment used, skills, and duties.

Job Description Statement of the tasks, duties, and responsibilities of a designated position to be performed.

Job Evaluation Systematic process of determining the relative worth of jobs to establish which jobs should be paid more than other jobs within an organization.

Job Family Pay structure that groups similar jobs or functions and then designates several levels within that grouping.

Long-term Incentive Plans Plans typically 3 to 5 years in length which carry longer term goals with greater payouts at or near the end of the plan term.

Management Plans Incentive or bonus plans for which only management or high-level individual contributors are eligible to participate. Usually includes company and individual objectives.

Manager's Compensation Guide Written manual provided to managers that covers all aspects of an organization's compensation program from philosophy to policies and procedures. The Guide also includes all tasks, responsibilities and forms to be used to execute all compensation programs.

Manufacturing or Production Plans Incentive or bonus plans designed specifically for a manufacturing or production type environment and has measures specific to their area.

Market Adjustment Pay adjustment given to an employee whose pay rate is falling behind market when the market is moving faster than their pay increases.

Market-based Pay Pay structure in which each job is assigned a pay range based on market benchmarking.

Market Benchmark Analysis	Process of gathering relevant market pay data for an organization's positions and comparing it to employee salaries.
Market Benchmarking	Process of identifying competitive pay levels for jobs in the external market.
Market Data	Pay rates obtained for jobs typically derived from salary surveys.
Market Data Guidelines	Compensation philosophy for each employee group and salary survey scopes to be used for market pay comparisons.
Market Pricing Policy	Organizational position governing how the organization will apply scopes of data from salary studies.
Market Rate Analysis	Process whereby salary data is gathered for similar organizations in the company's industry, including number of employees, and applied using the same relative financial metric to determine average pay in the market for a position.
Market Reference Group	Process of combining market benchmarking value for 4 or 5 similar jobs to get an average market value for a position for which individual market benchmarking data cannot be obtained.
MBOs (Management by Objectives)	Management methodology which relies on the inclusion, performance and measurement of goals in an incentive or bonus plan.
Merit Budget	Pool of money designated to be used for employee merit pay increases (which are typically based on performance).
Merit Dollars	Money budgeted within an organization for employee merit increases.
Merit Pay	Pay increase typically based on measurements of an employee's performance.
Millennials	Term describing the age group of a person typically born between 1981 and the late 1990's. Also known as "Generation Y."
Mission Statement	Statement that typically describes the purpose of what an organization does, for whom they do it, and how they do it.

Glossary

Nonexempt/ Exempt Employees	Exemption status of an employee which determines who will or will not receive overtime payments under the *Fair Labor Standards Act (FLSA)*.
Pay Compression	Situation when only a small difference in pay exists between employees regardless of experience or skills. See also *Wage-Rate Compression*.
Pay Grades/Bands	Groups of jobs paid within the same pay range or band.
Pay System Review	Analysis conducted to ensure your pay grade mid-points are keeping up with the market, and that jobs of similar market value or internal equity value are in the same pay range.
Process Transparency	Compensation philosophy and practice in which information is shared with employees about the company's compensation system from a process-only perspective (i.e., from where benchmark is derived, pay scale for their job only, etc.)
Profit Sharing	Any incentive plan by which an employer pays, or makes available to all employees, payments based on company profits.
Qualifying Exemption Classification	Exemption classification for each employee as determined by an employer according to *Fair Labor Standards Act (FLSA)* guidelines.
Reasonable Accommodation	Adjustment made in an employment or compensation system to make that system fair for an individual based on a proven need. Typically, accommodations can be religious, academic, or employment-related. Often, they are mandated by law.
Reward-to-performance Ratio	Amount of performance effort required to earn a reward. Typically, the reward-to-performance ratio attempts to align the reward with the amount of performance that must be achieved to earn the award.
Salary Surveys	Independent third-party studies that compile pay information typically for a specific industry or employer size. Also referred to as *Wage and Salary Surveys*.
Sales Compensation	Compensation earned by a salesperson in base pay as well as any sales incentives, bonuses or commissions received.

Sales Compensation Plans	Plans that reward direct sales employees for their performance with bonuses, incentives, or commissions.
Shift Premium	Additional pay provided to an employee for working a second or third shift.
Short-term Incentive Plans	Incentive or bonus plans that are one year or less in duration.
Skill/Knowledge-based Pay	Pay structure where pay is specific to an individual employee based on how many skills or how much knowledge they acquire.
SMART Goals	Methodology used to establish goals wherein each goal is to be specific, measurable, achievable, realistic, and time-related.
Step Pay	Pay structure where pay adjustments are made based on time-in-job.
Stretch Goals	Typically, a goal that requires employees to go "above and beyond" to attain it. Stretch goals are not easy to attain; nor are they extremely difficult to attain.
Stock Plans	Type of incentive plan that rewards employees in the form of stock which can later be converted to cash.
Survey Matching	Process by which an employer compares a position's job description to the job description from a survey for purposes of submitting data for the survey and using the data when the survey is complete.
Target Mix	Targeted pay mix an employer desires an employee to obtain between base pay and incentive pay. For example, 60/40 means the target pay mix is 60% base pay and 40% incentive pay.
Team Plans	Incentive or bonus plans designed specifically to include goals and measures a team can truly influence and attain.
Threshold Performance Levels	Goal level on each performance-based objective that must be attained to earn some portion of the pay reward assigned to it.
Total Compensation Review	Analysis focused on all employee compensation programs. Compare to *Total Rewards Review*.

Total Rewards Review — Analysis focused on all employee rewards programs, including but not limited to compensation, benefits, wellness, work/life, etc. Compare to *Total Compensation Review.*

Total Target Cash — Targeted dollar amount including base and bonus pay, incentives, or commissions an employer desires an employee to earn in their role.

Total Rewards — Everything an employee values in their employment relationship including compensation, benefits, wellness initiatives, work/life programs, time-off, etc.

Total Rewards Philosophy — Statement that typically describes how an organization wishes to value and utilize various components of total rewards (compensation, benefits, wellness initiatives, work/life programs, time-off, etc.) as it relates to the organization's culture.

Total Rewards Strategic Assessment — Review of all things related to total rewards (including philosophy, policies, procedures, practices, goals, gaps to market, and desired future direction) compiled into a report with a "roadmap" and recommendations for updating and revising the total rewards program.

Traditionalists — Term describing the age group of a person typically born between 1928 and 1945.

Variable Pay — At-risk pay that must be re-earned during each measurable period as designated in an incentive or bonus plan.

Wage and Salary Survey — See *Salary Surveys.*

Wage-Rate Compression — Situation when only a small difference in pay exists between job levels, specifically between hourly employees and their direct managers. See also *Pay Compression.*

Weighting Factors — Factors or objectives that influence plan payments. See also *Weights.*

Weights — Percentages assigned to each *Weighting Factor.*

Upside Potential — Typically, a ratio (e.g., 2:1), that indicates how much a salesperson can earn beyond their base target compensation in a total payout on their plan. Thus, a 2:1 plan is said to have a 2:1 upside potential.

CPSIA information can be obtained
at www.ICGtesting.com
Printed in the USA
LVHW050328241219
641493LV00027BA/534/P